Mandalas Adult Coloring Book
Stress Less Coloring

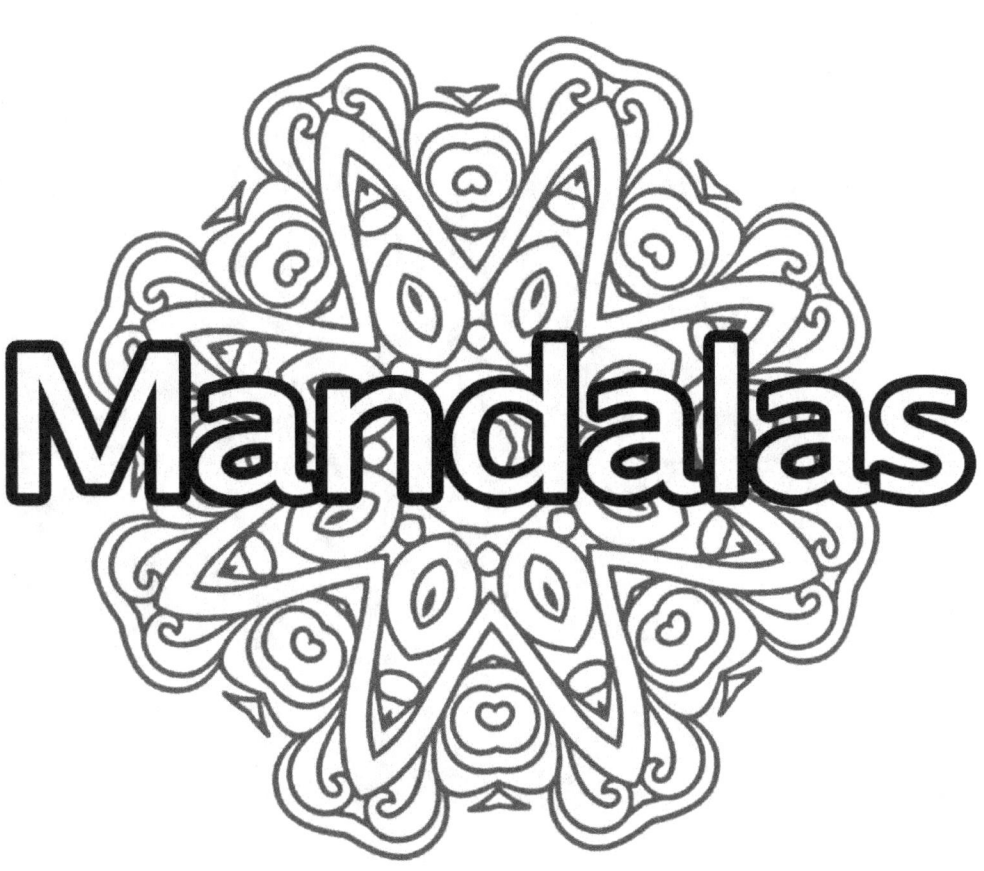

Jasmine Andrews

Mandalas Adult Coloring Book
Stress Less Coloring

Copyright: Published in the United States by Jasmine Andrews
Published March 2017

All rights reserved. No part of this publication may be reproduced, stored in retrieval system, copied in any form or by any means, electronic, mechanical, photocopying, recording or otherwise transmitted without written permission from the publisher. Please do not participate in or encourage piracy of this material in any way. You must not circulate this book in any format. Jasmine Andrews *does not control or direct users' actions and is not responsible for the information or content shared, harm and/or actions of the book readers.*

ISBN-13: 978-1544814858

ISBN-10: 1544814852

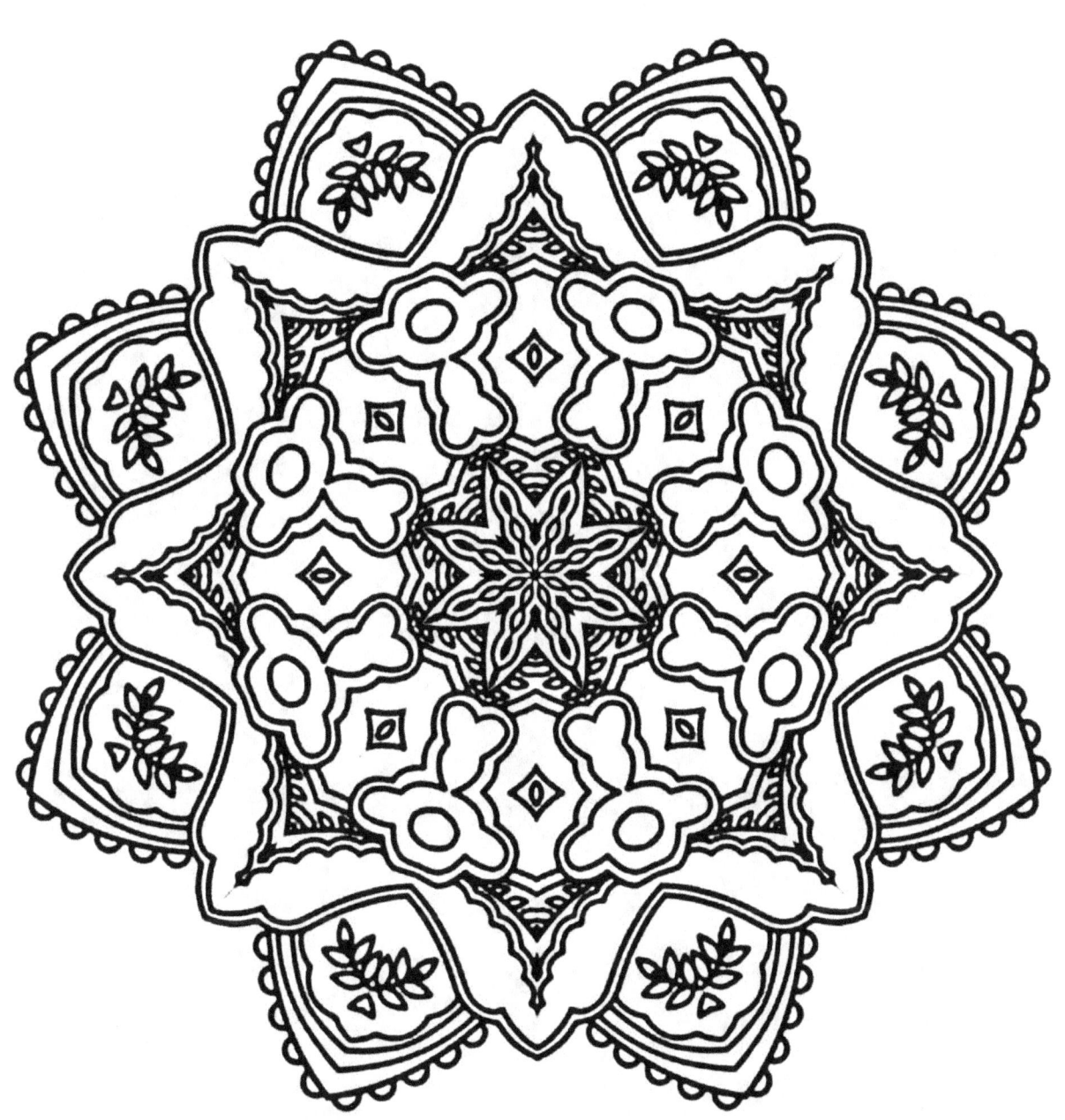

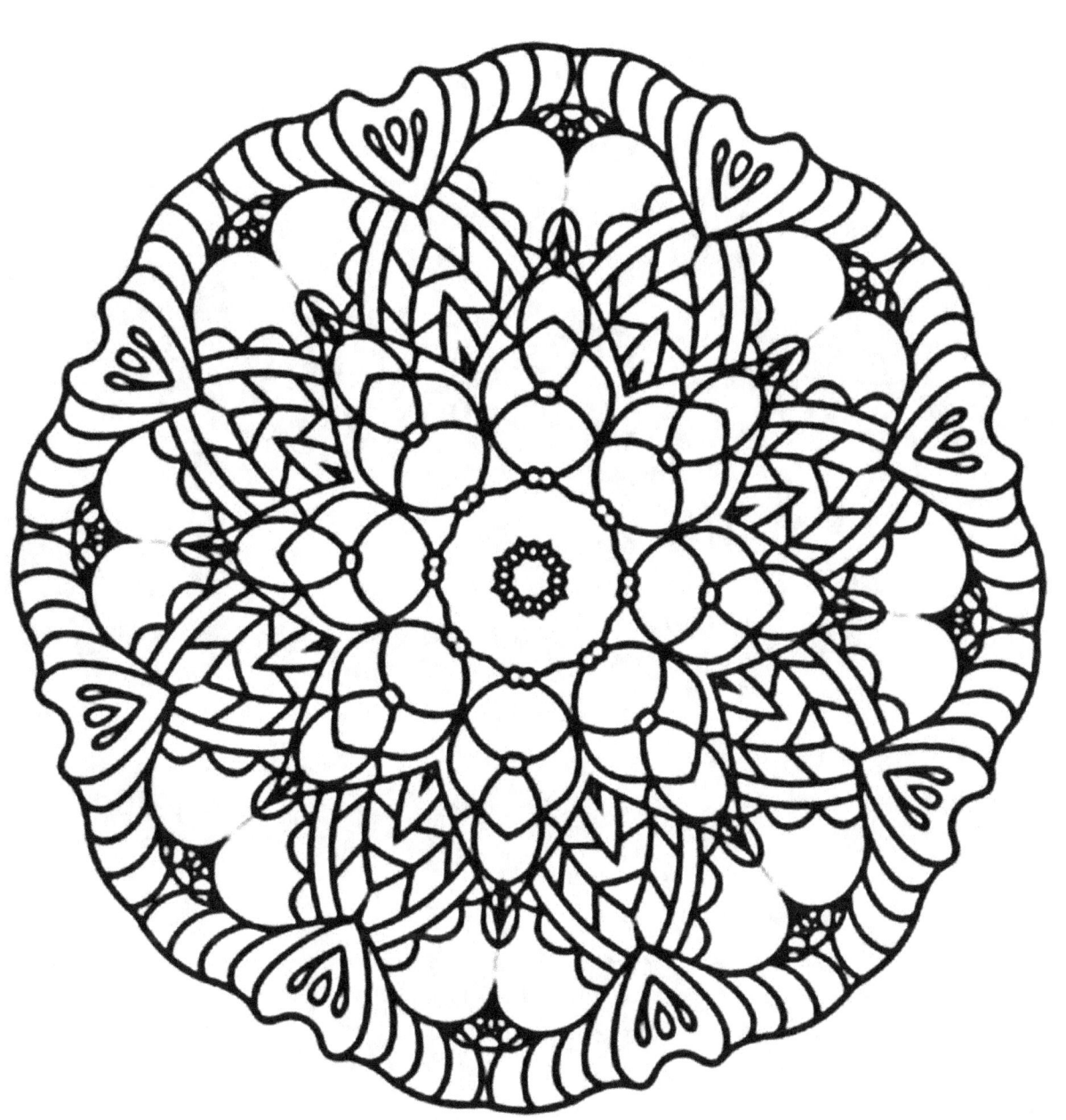

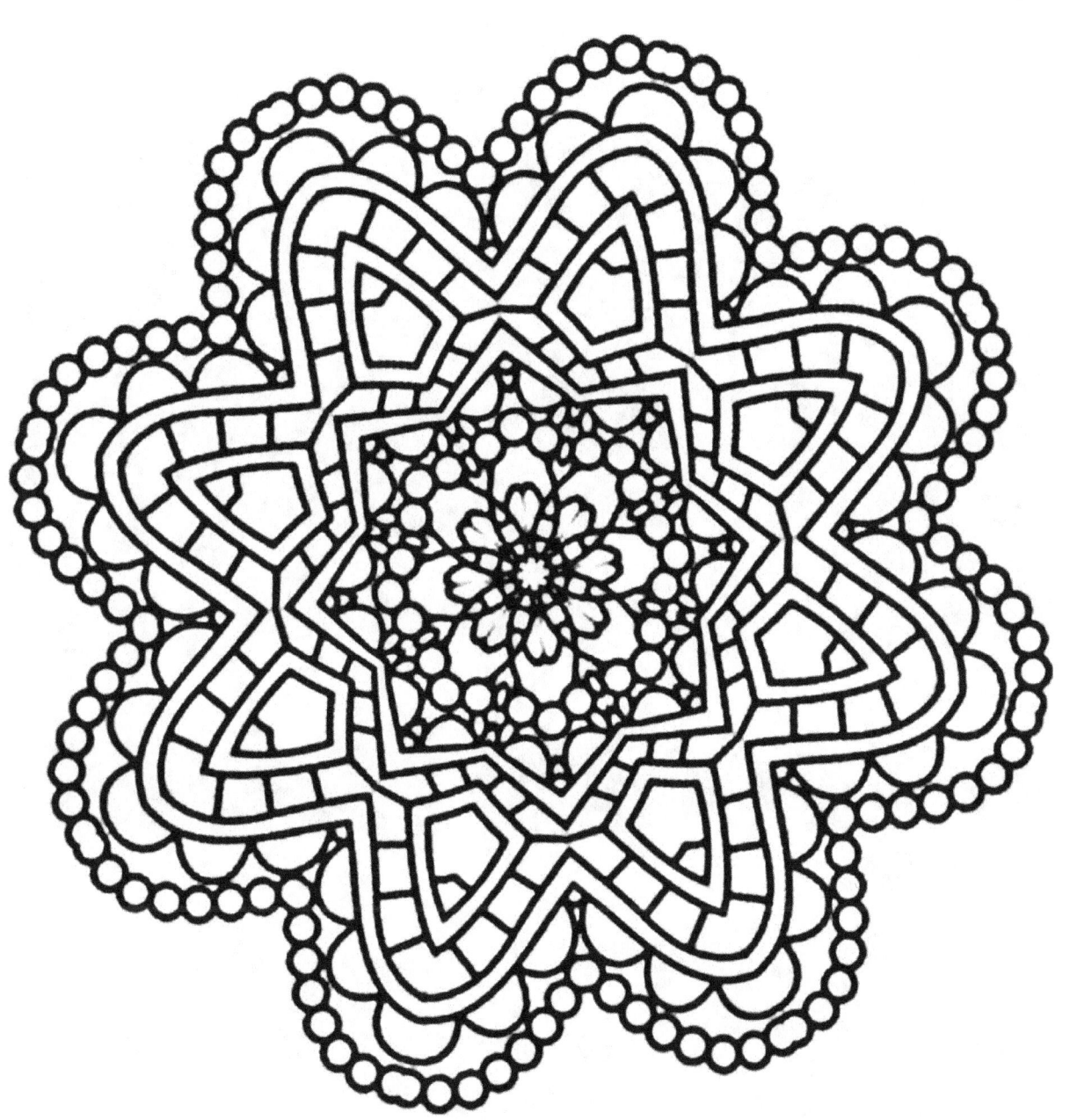

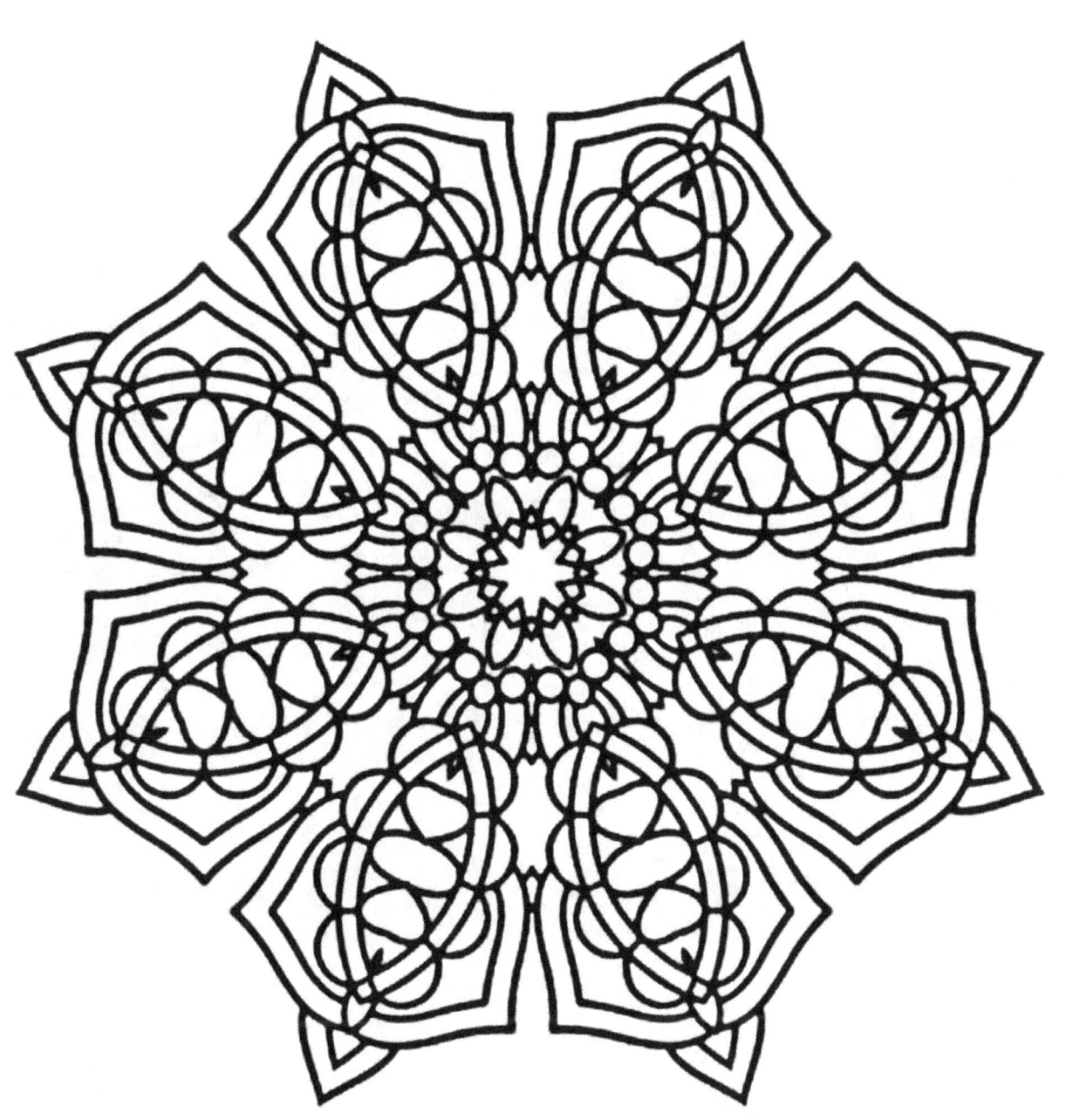

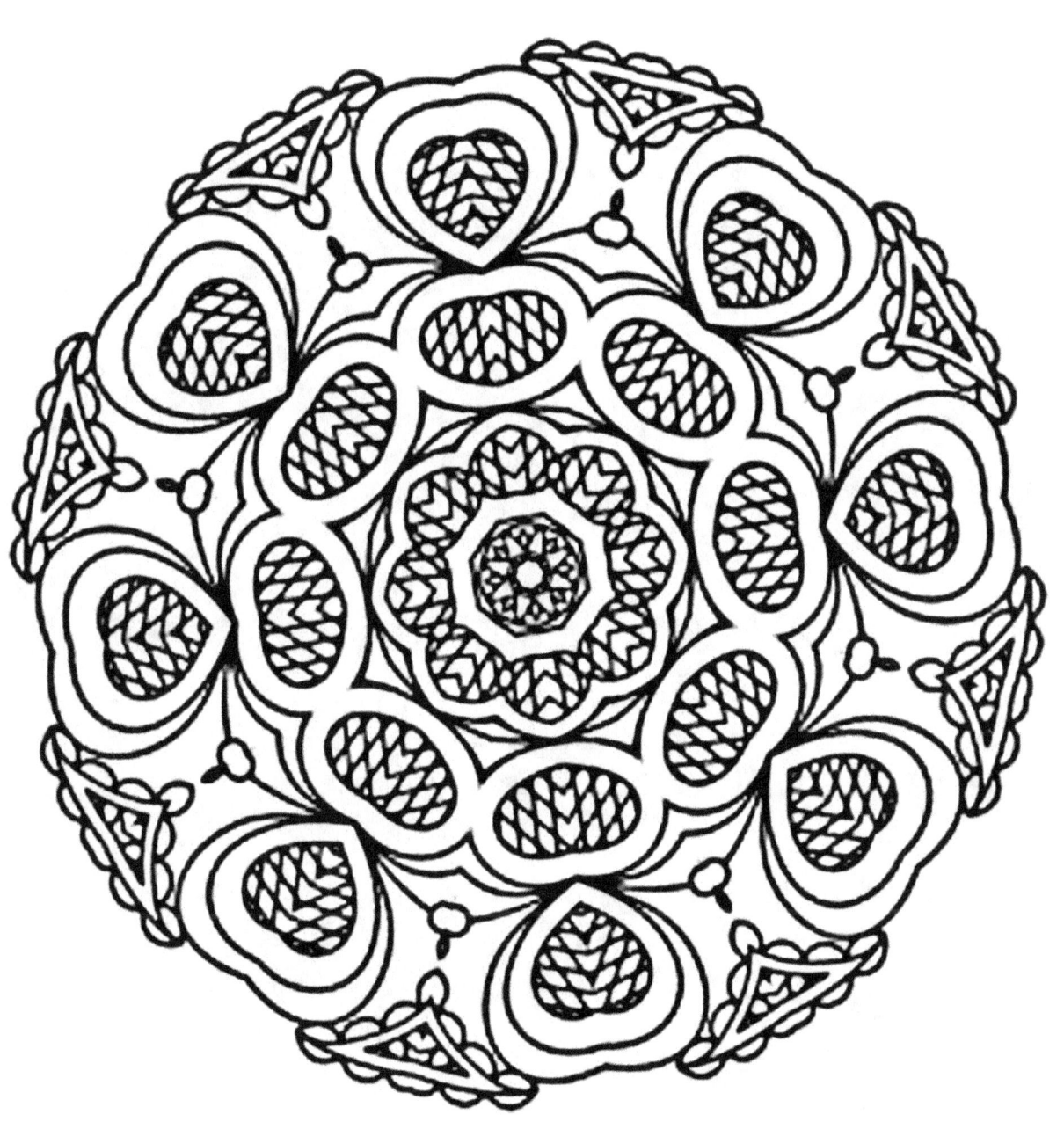

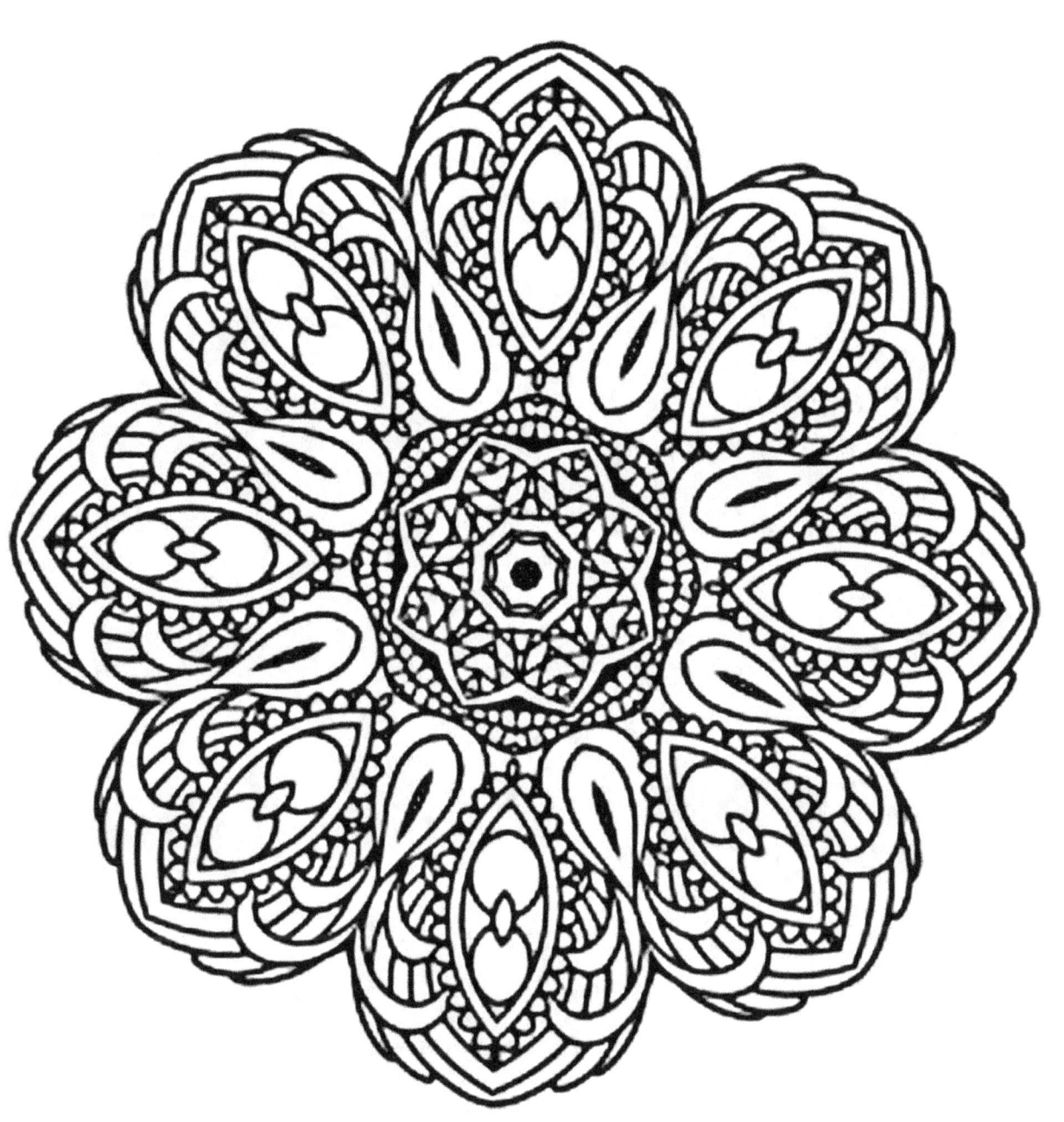

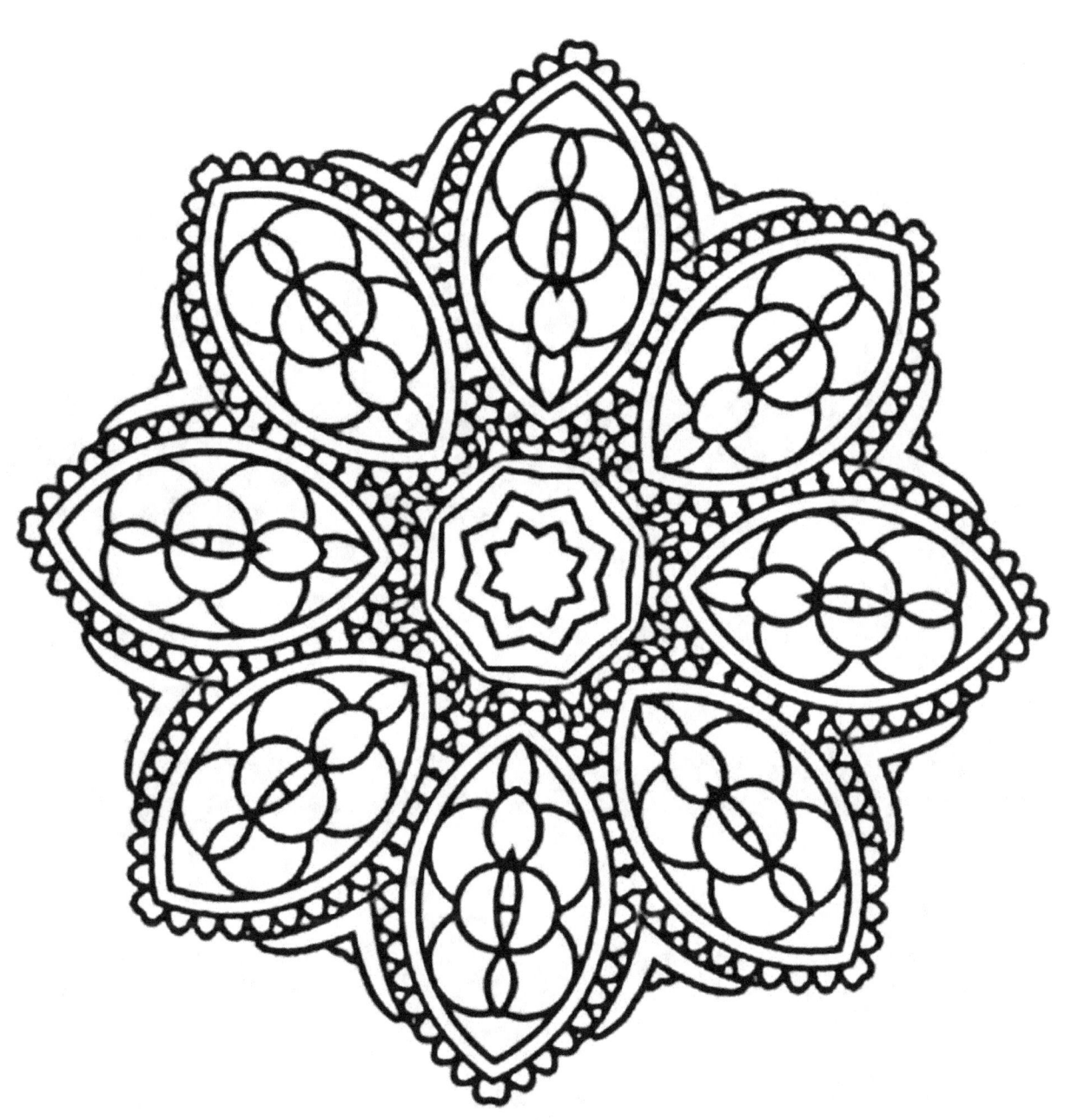

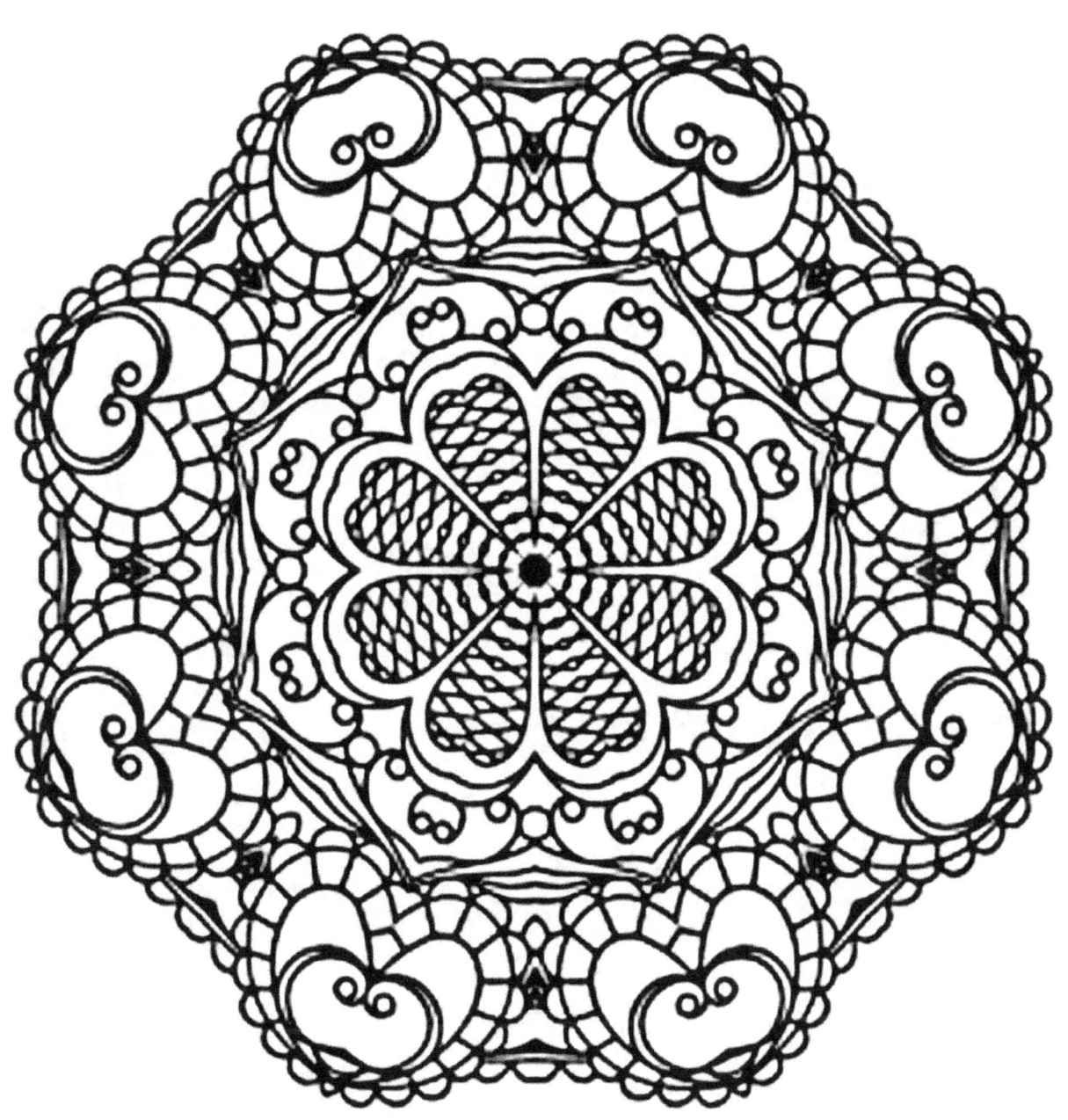

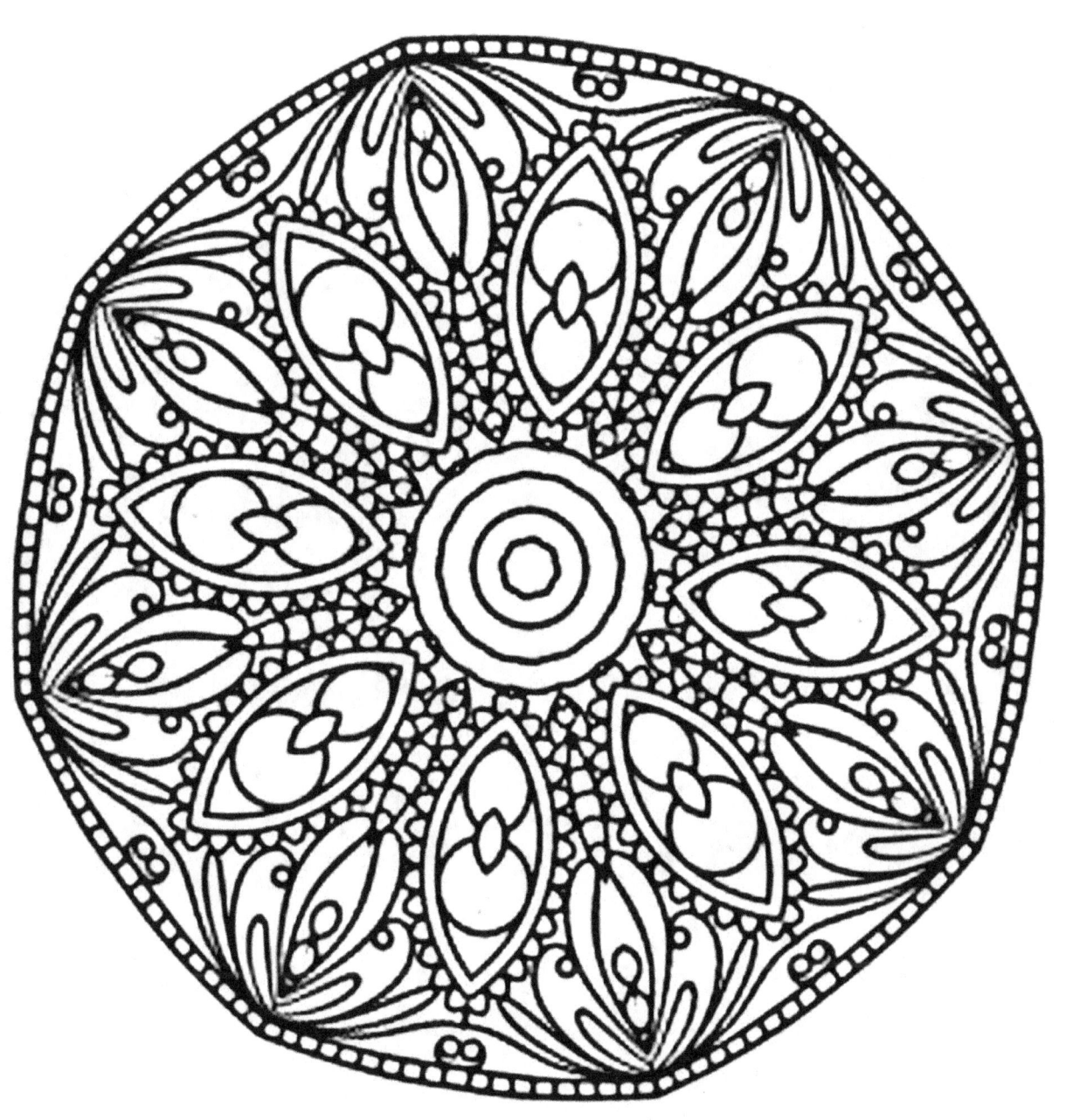

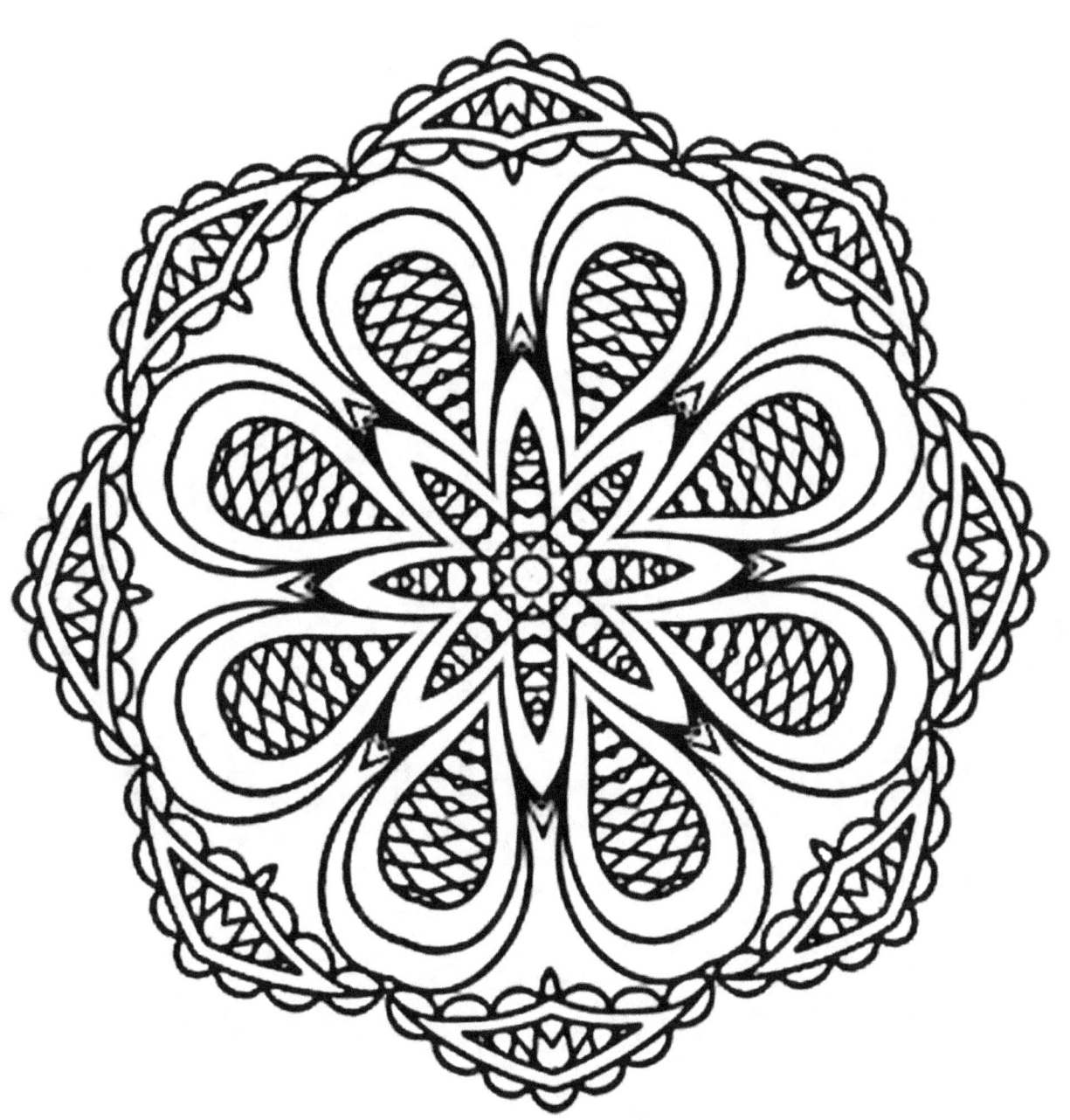

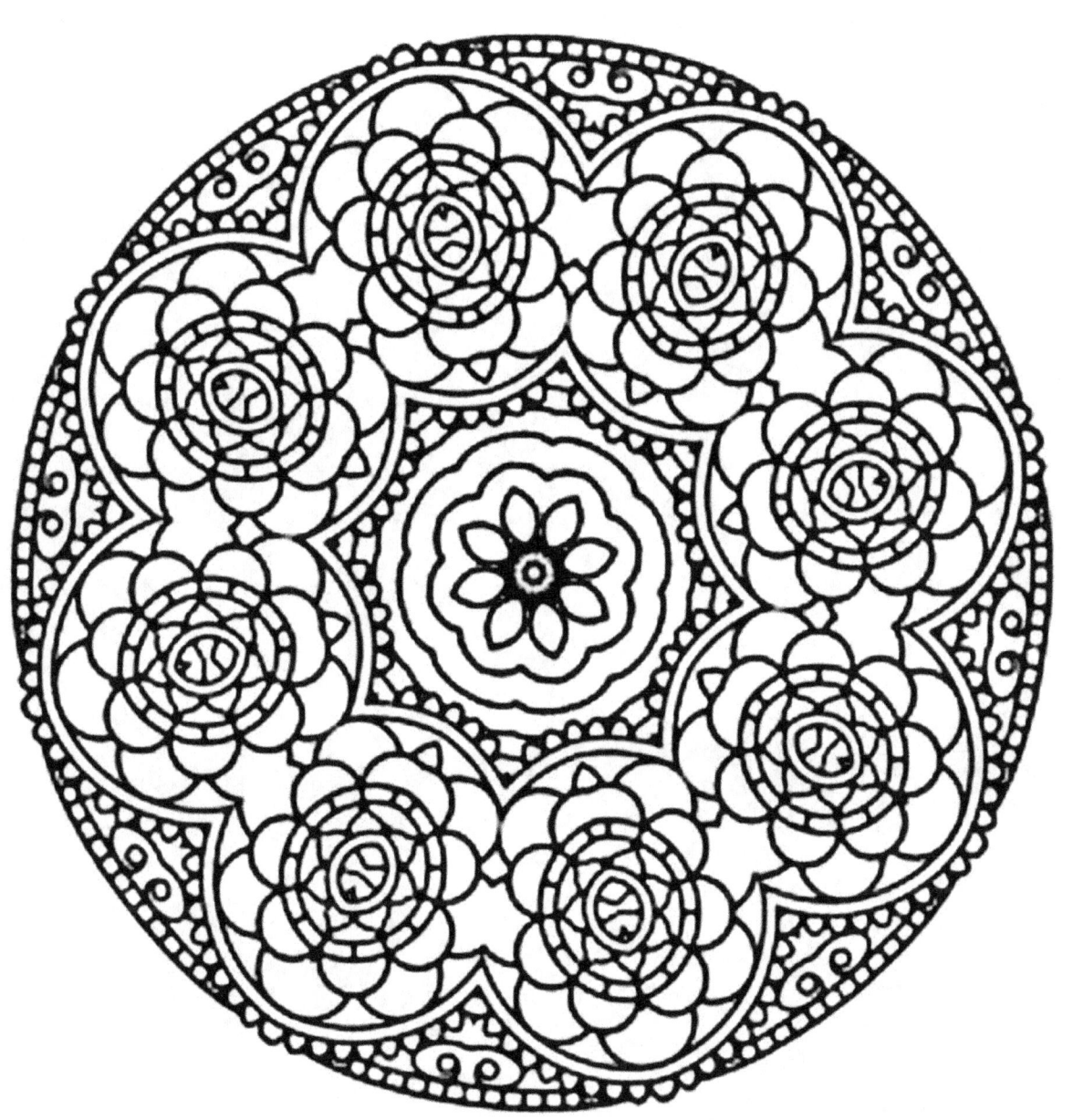

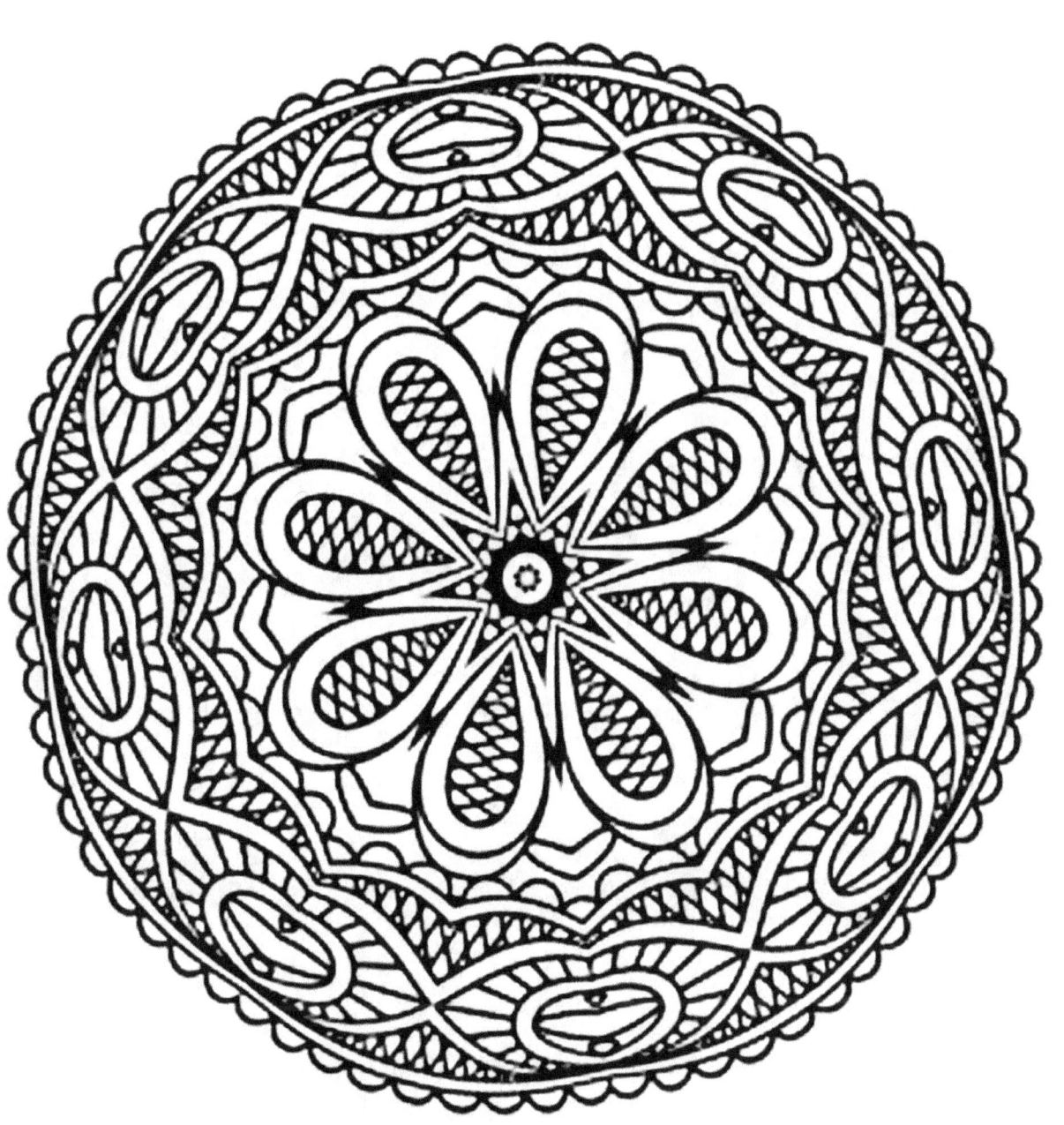

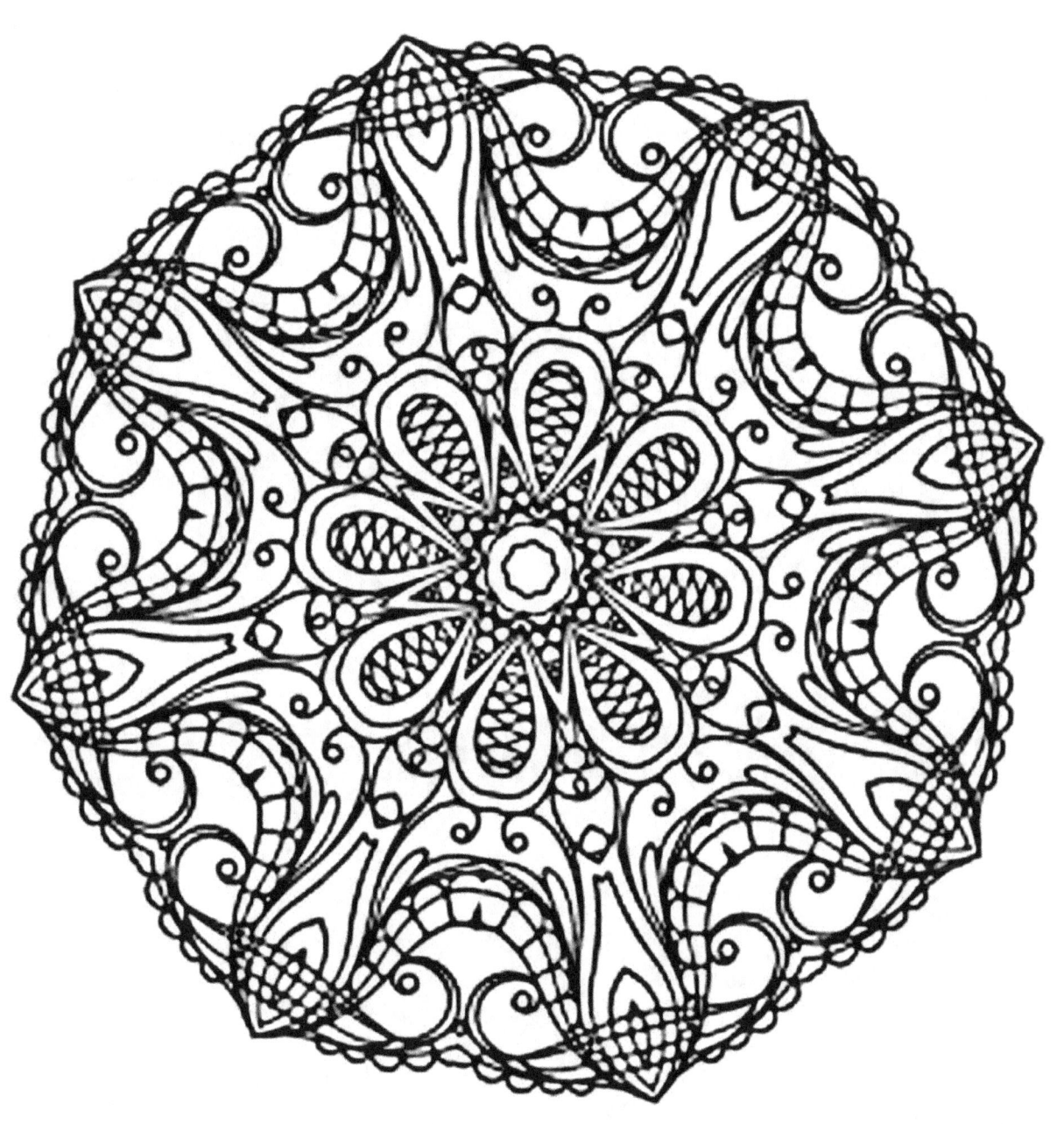

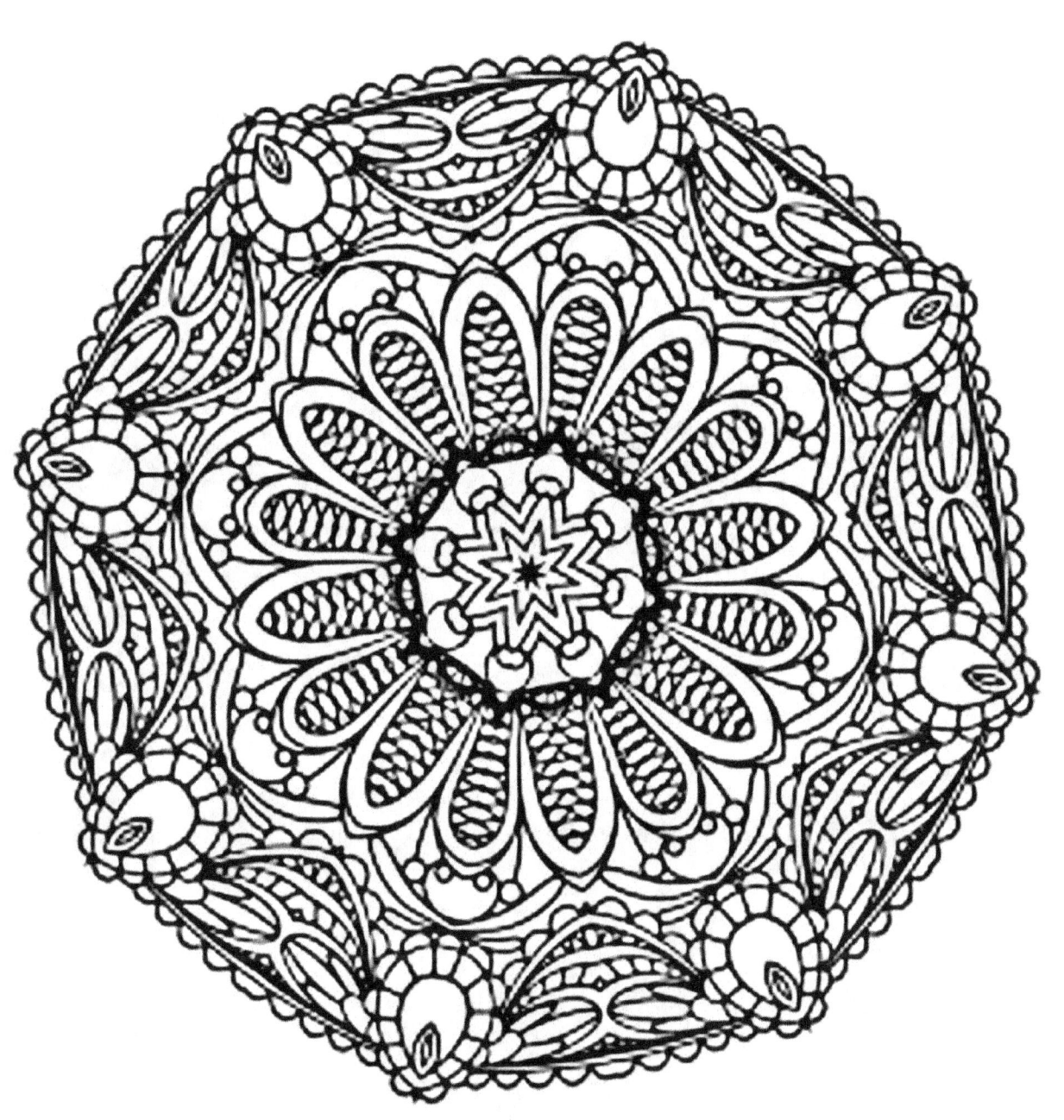

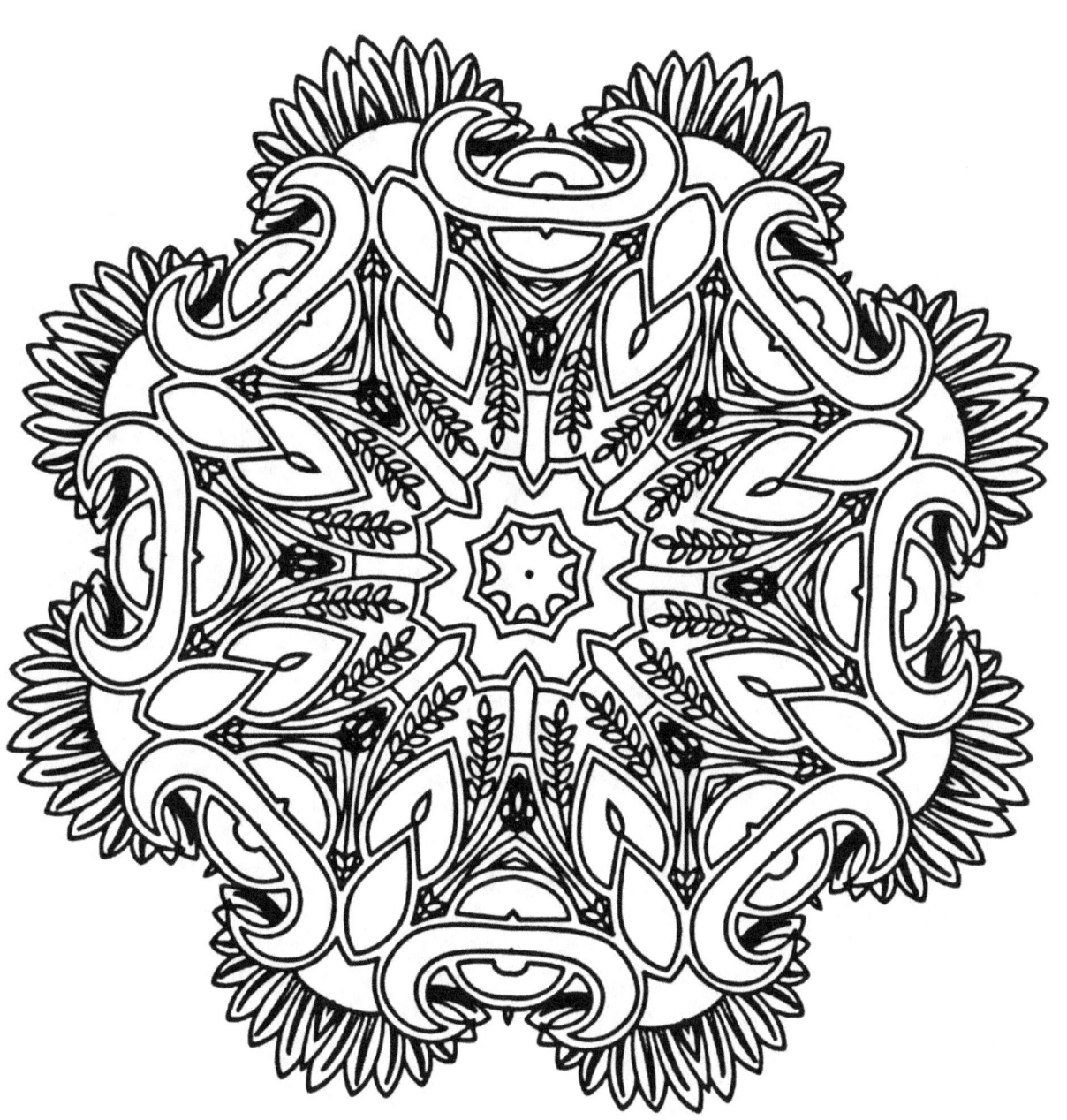

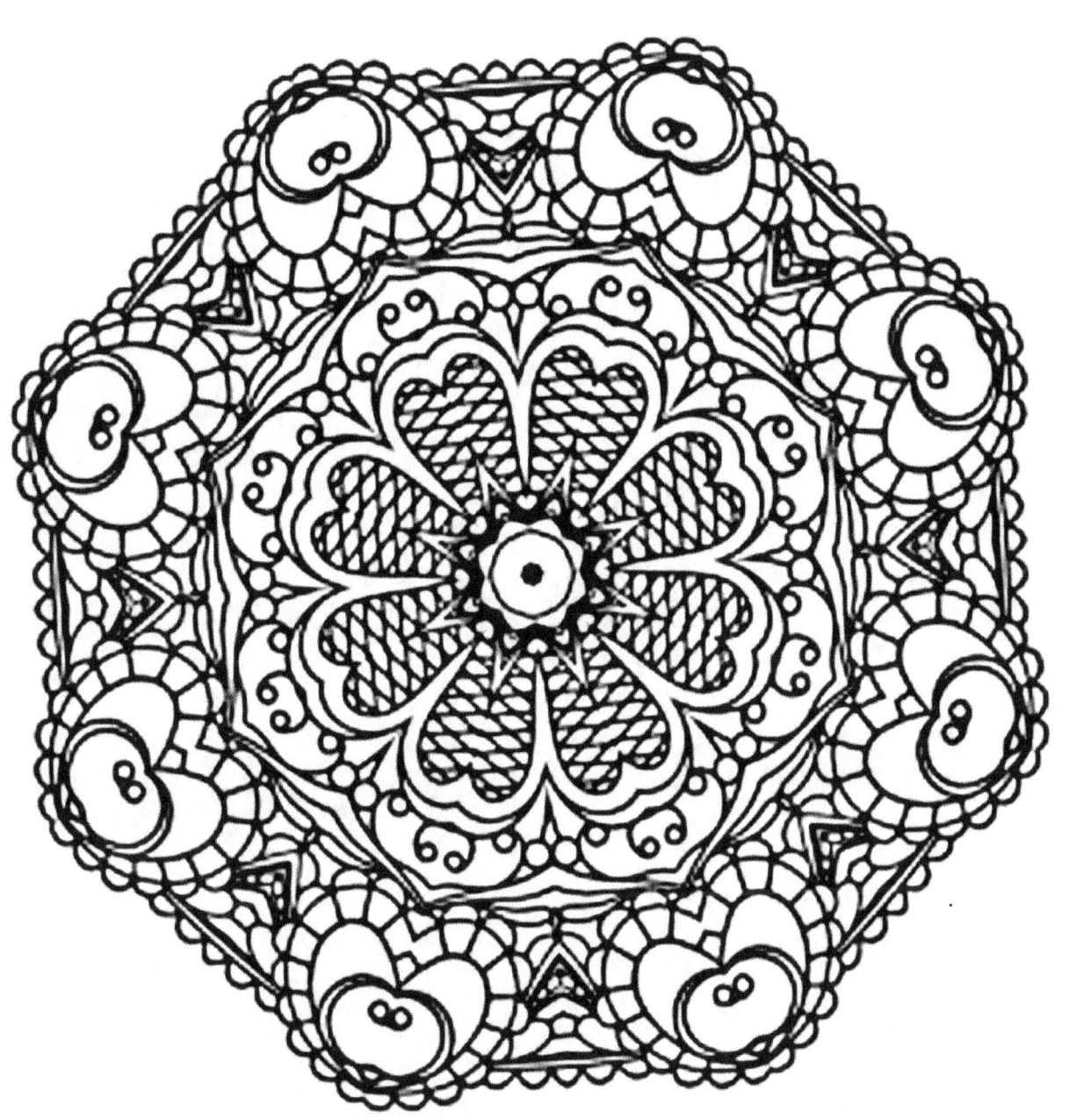

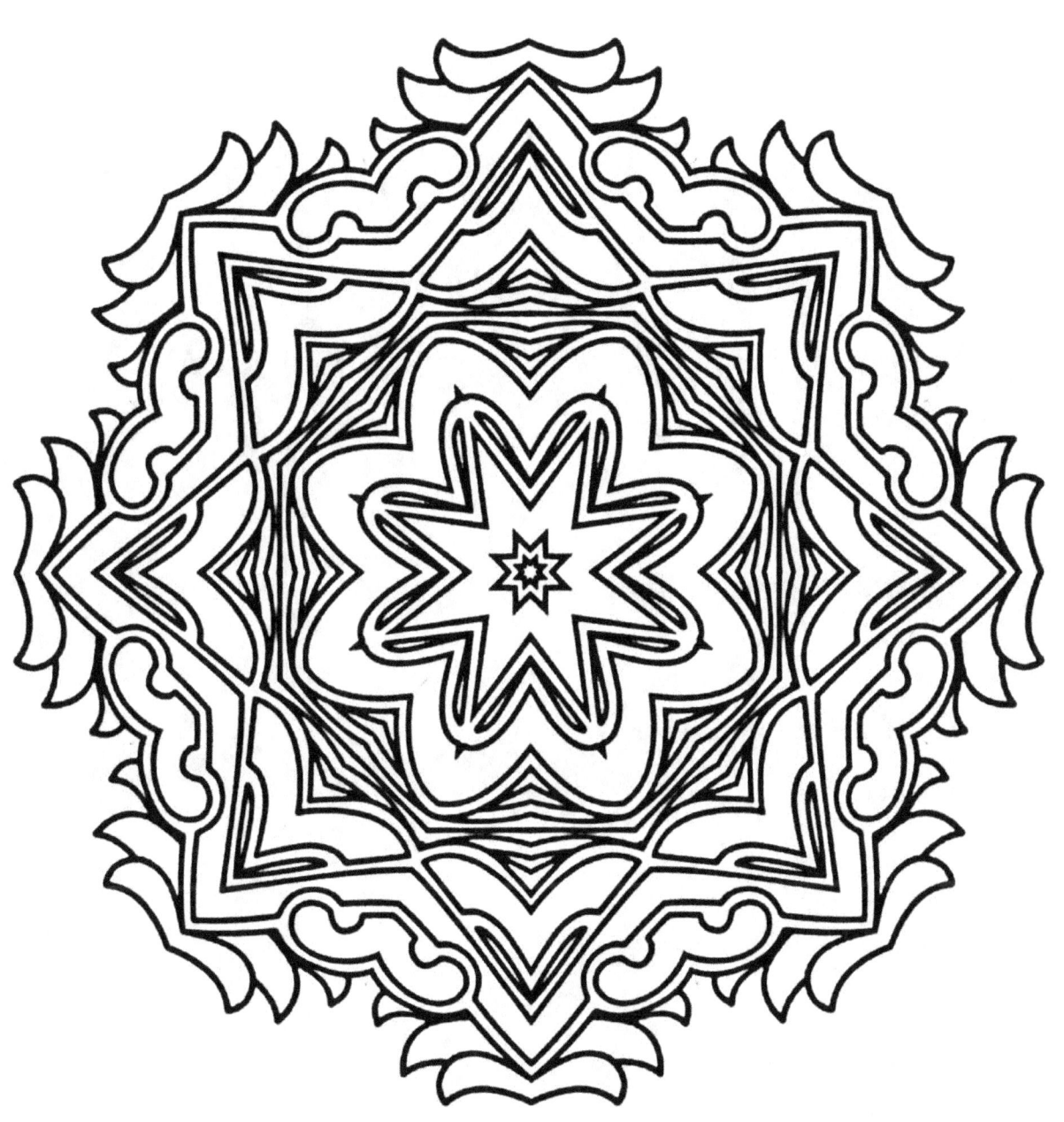

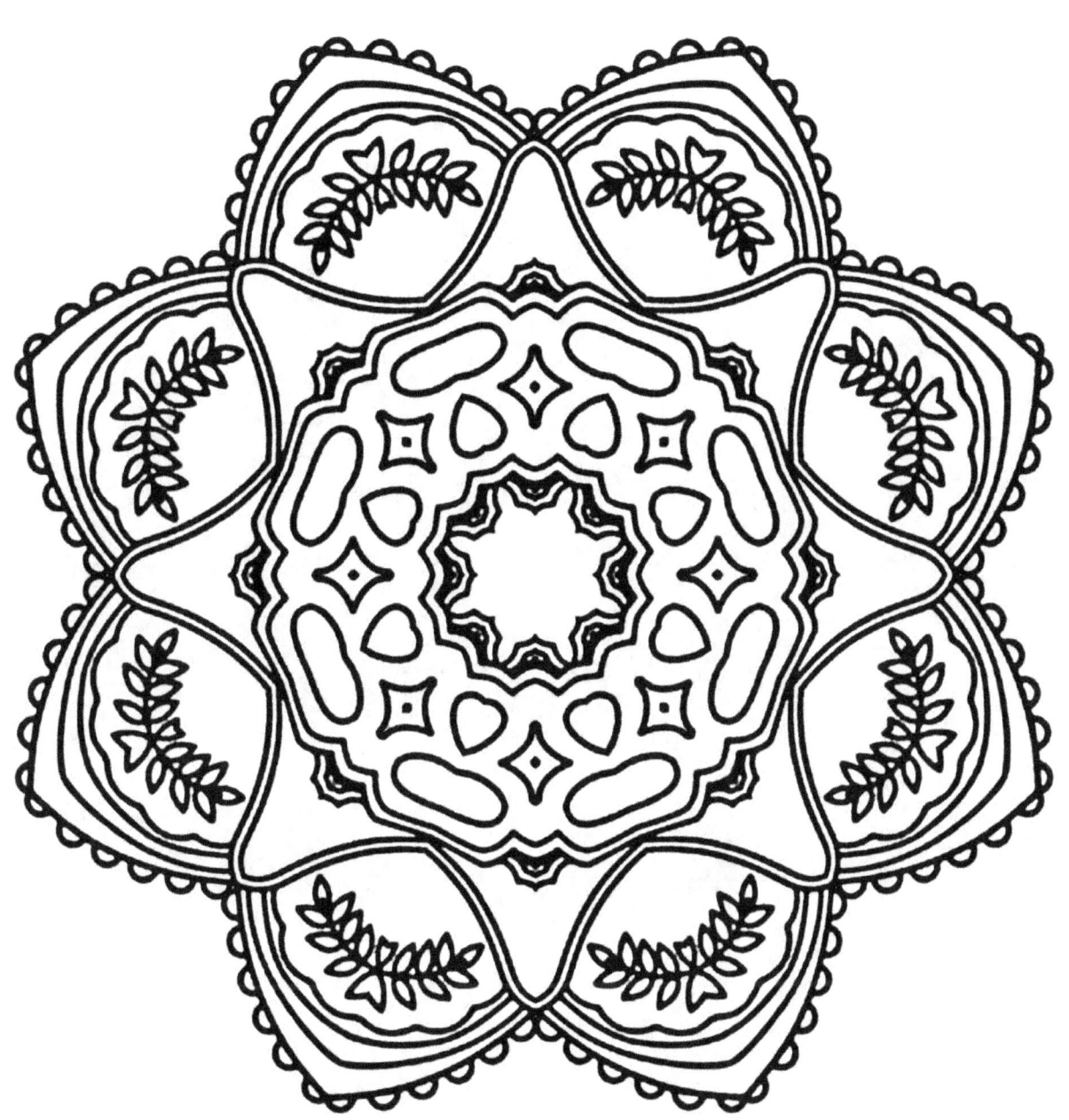

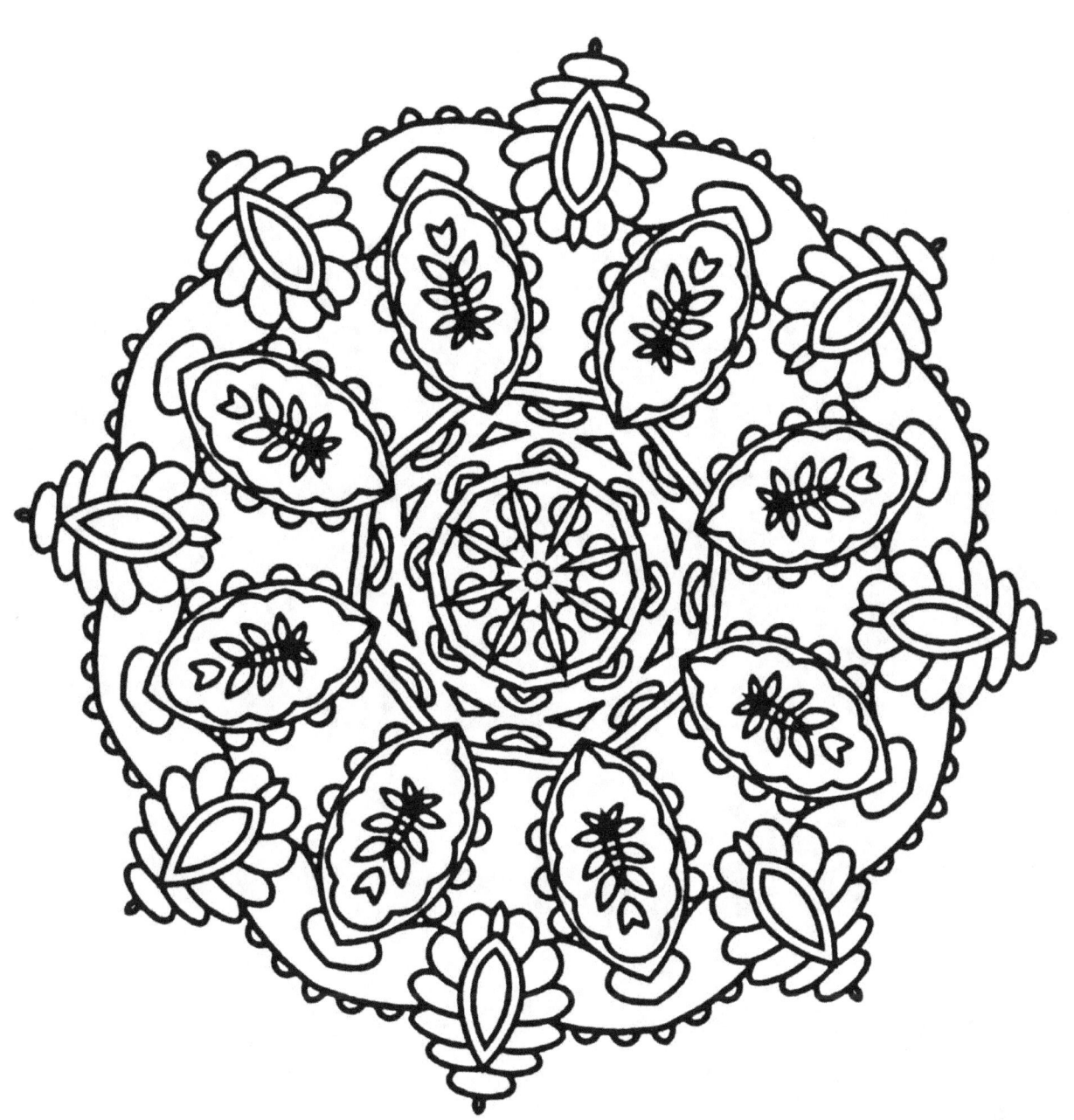

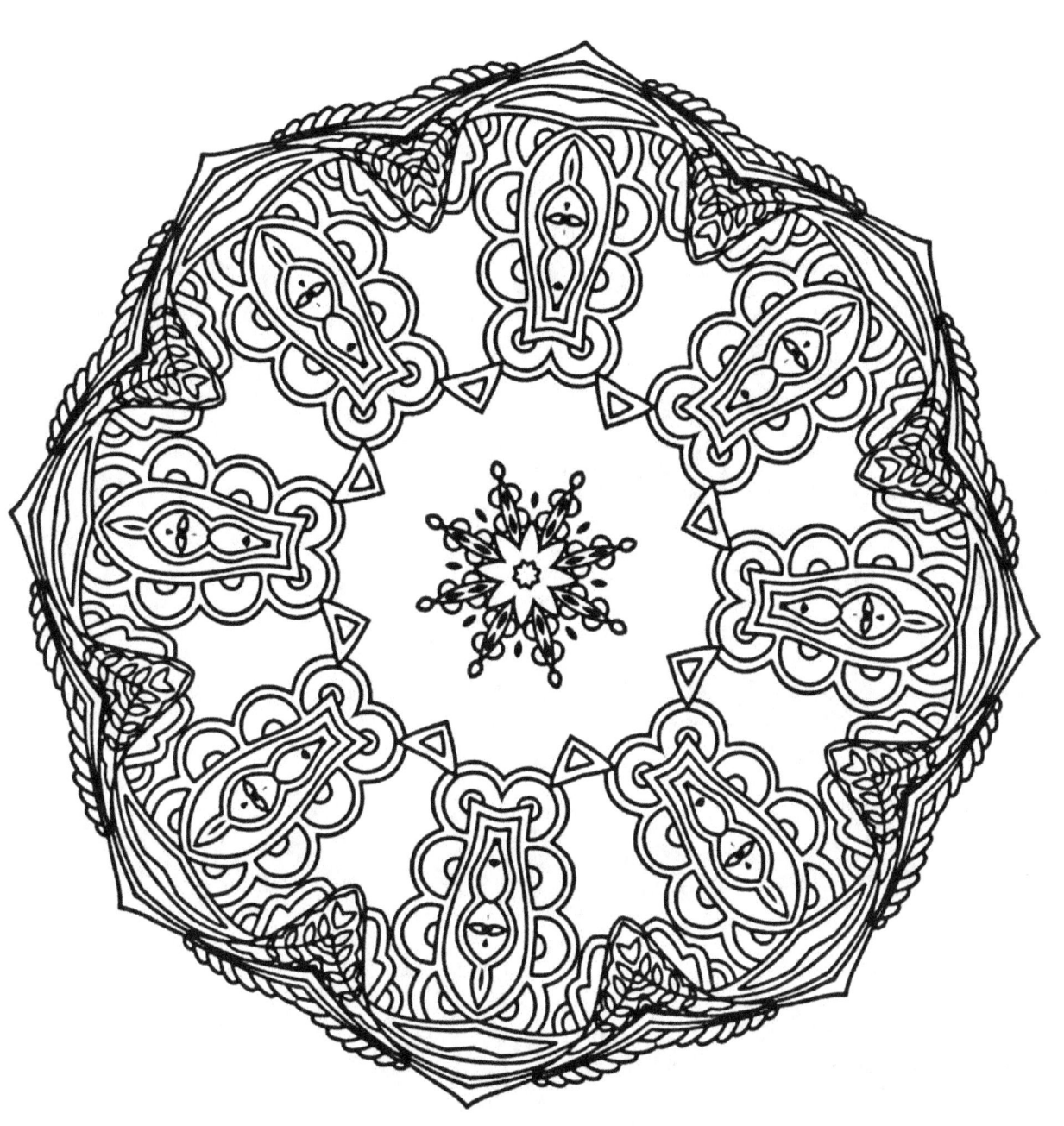

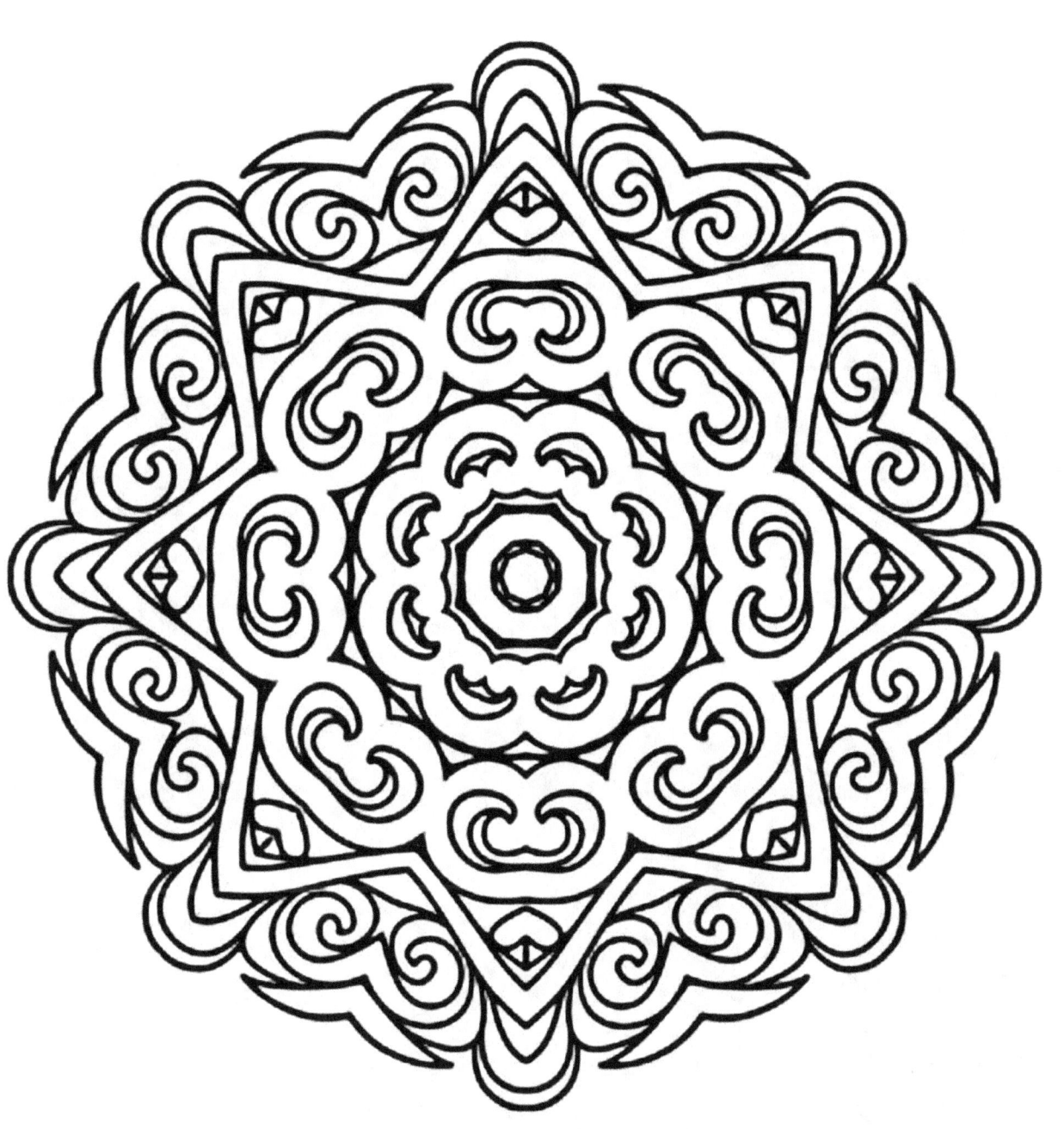

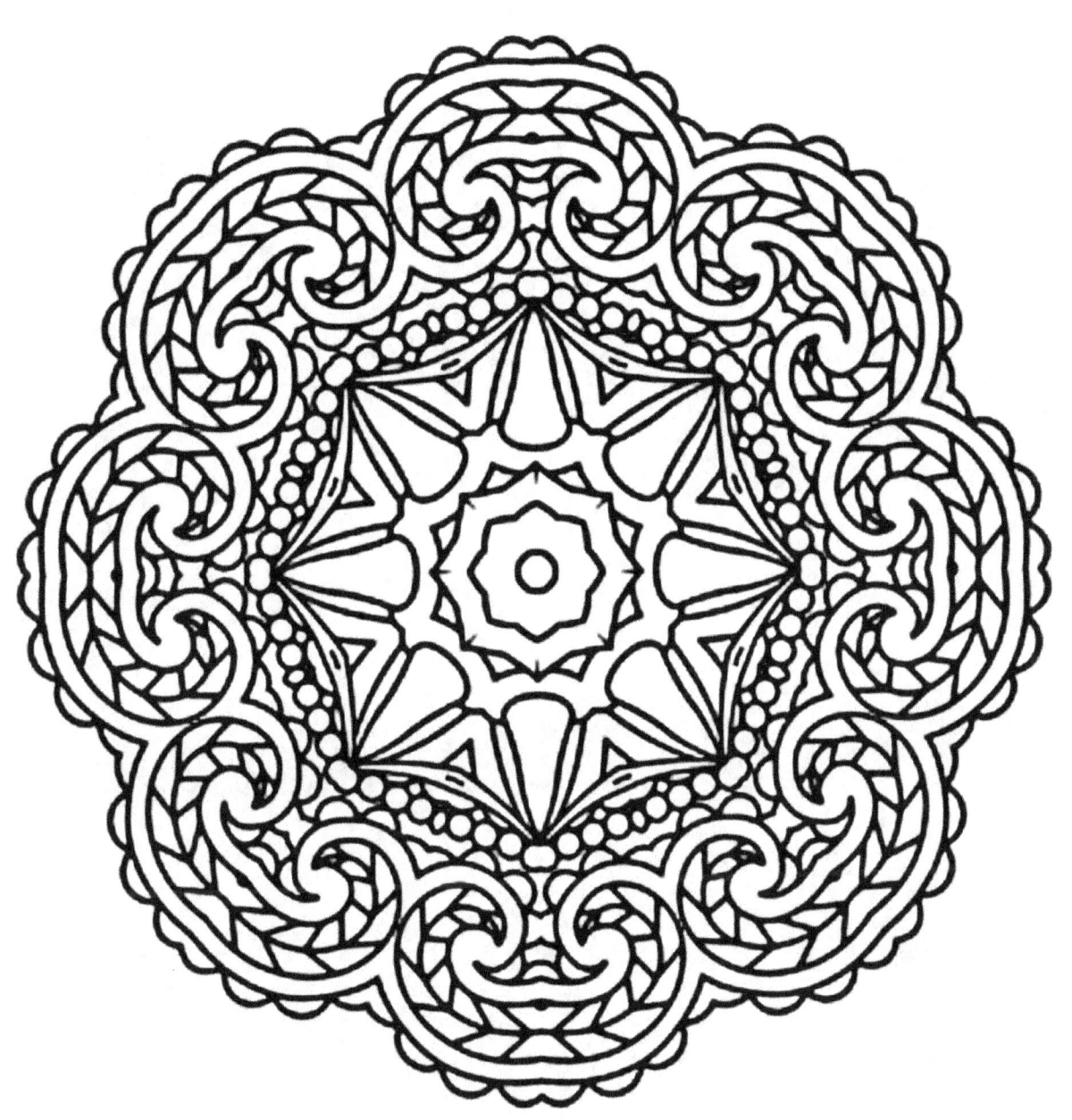

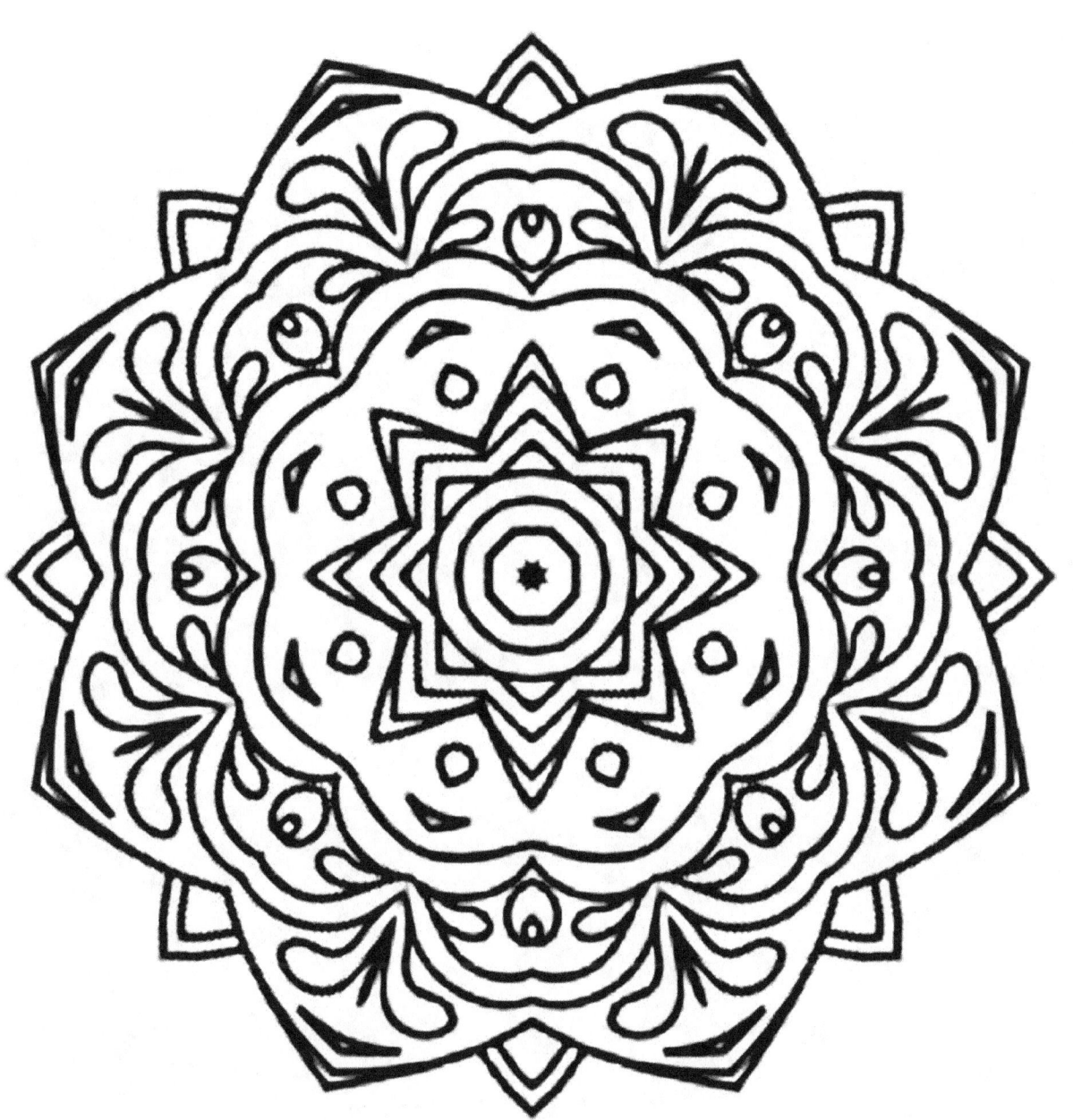

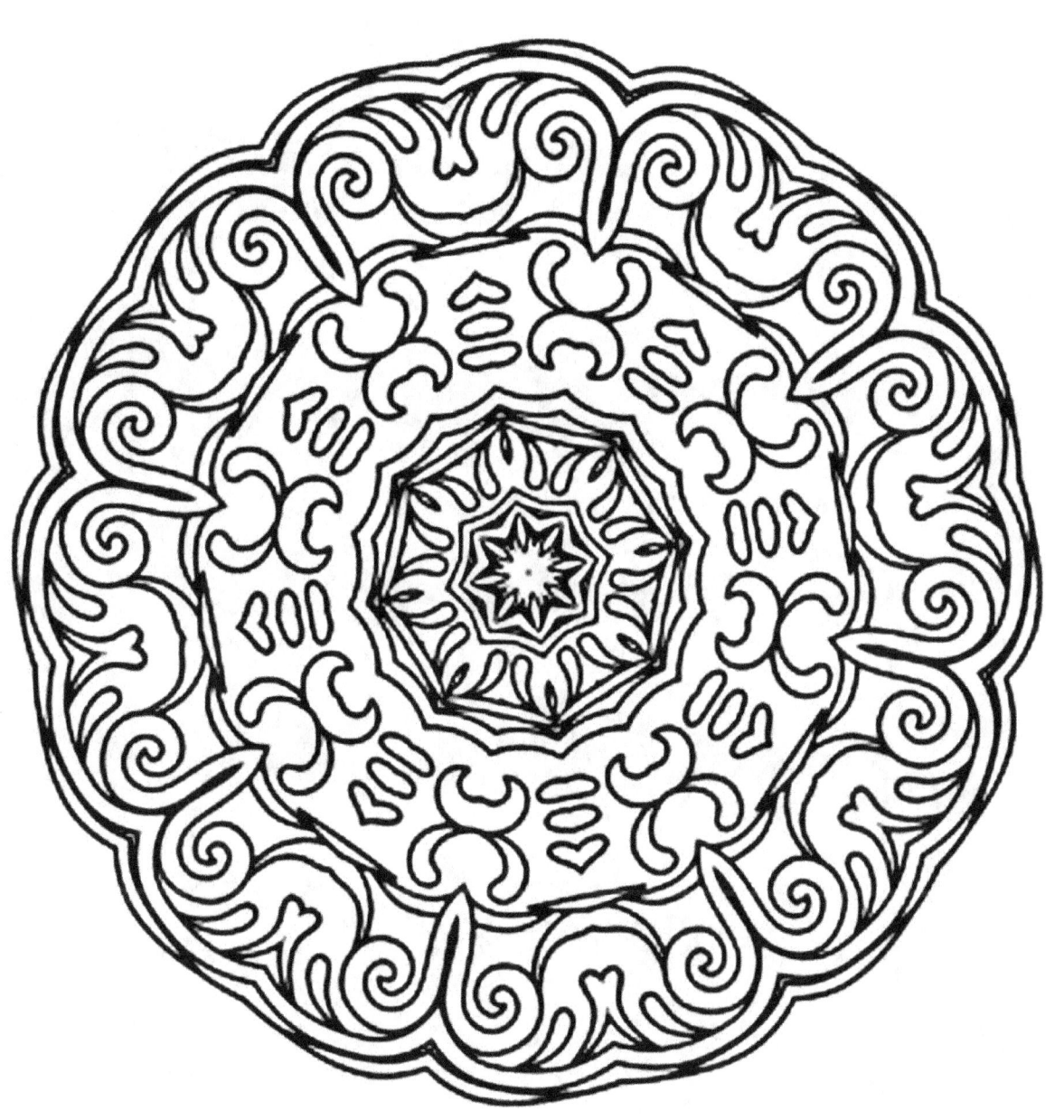

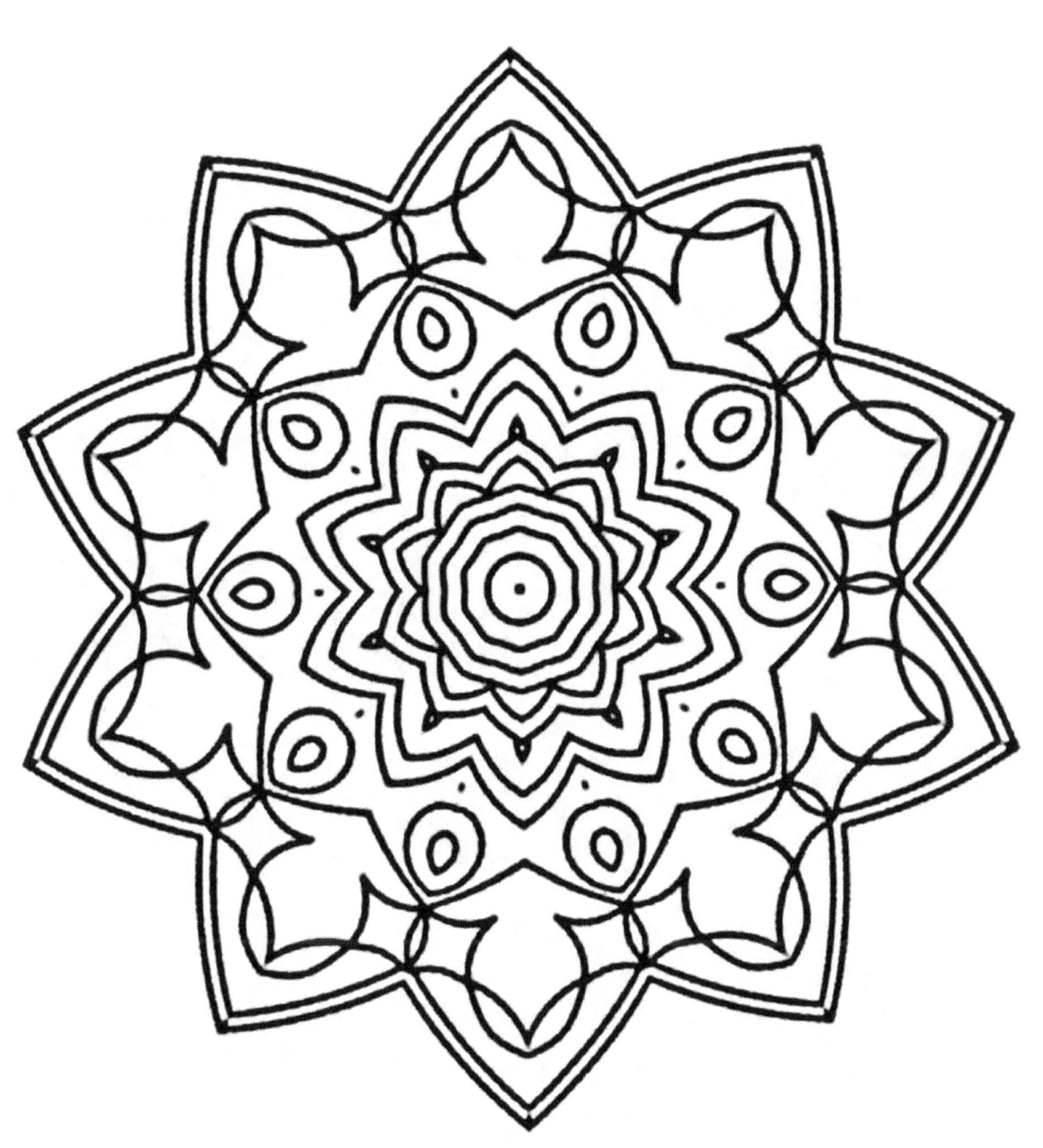

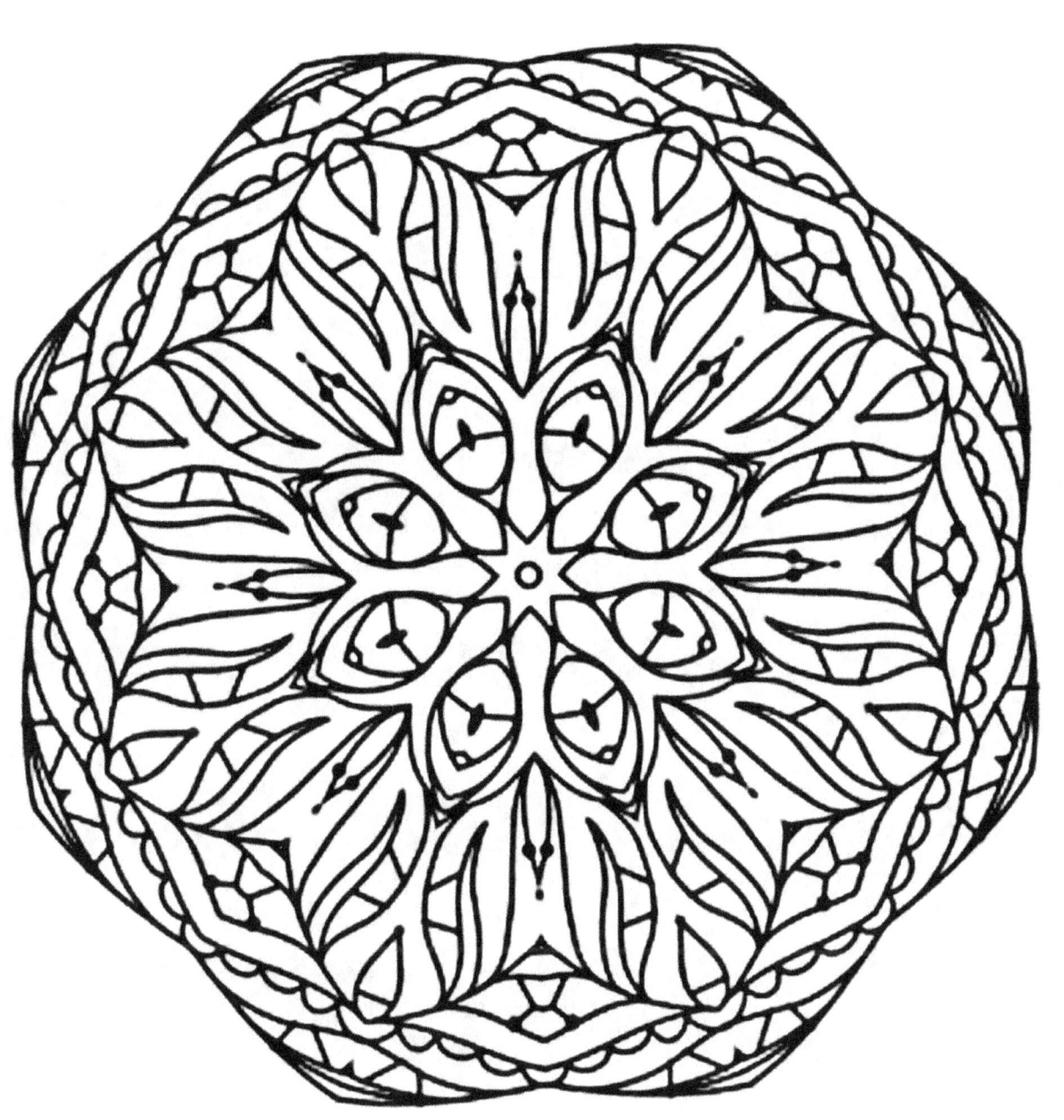

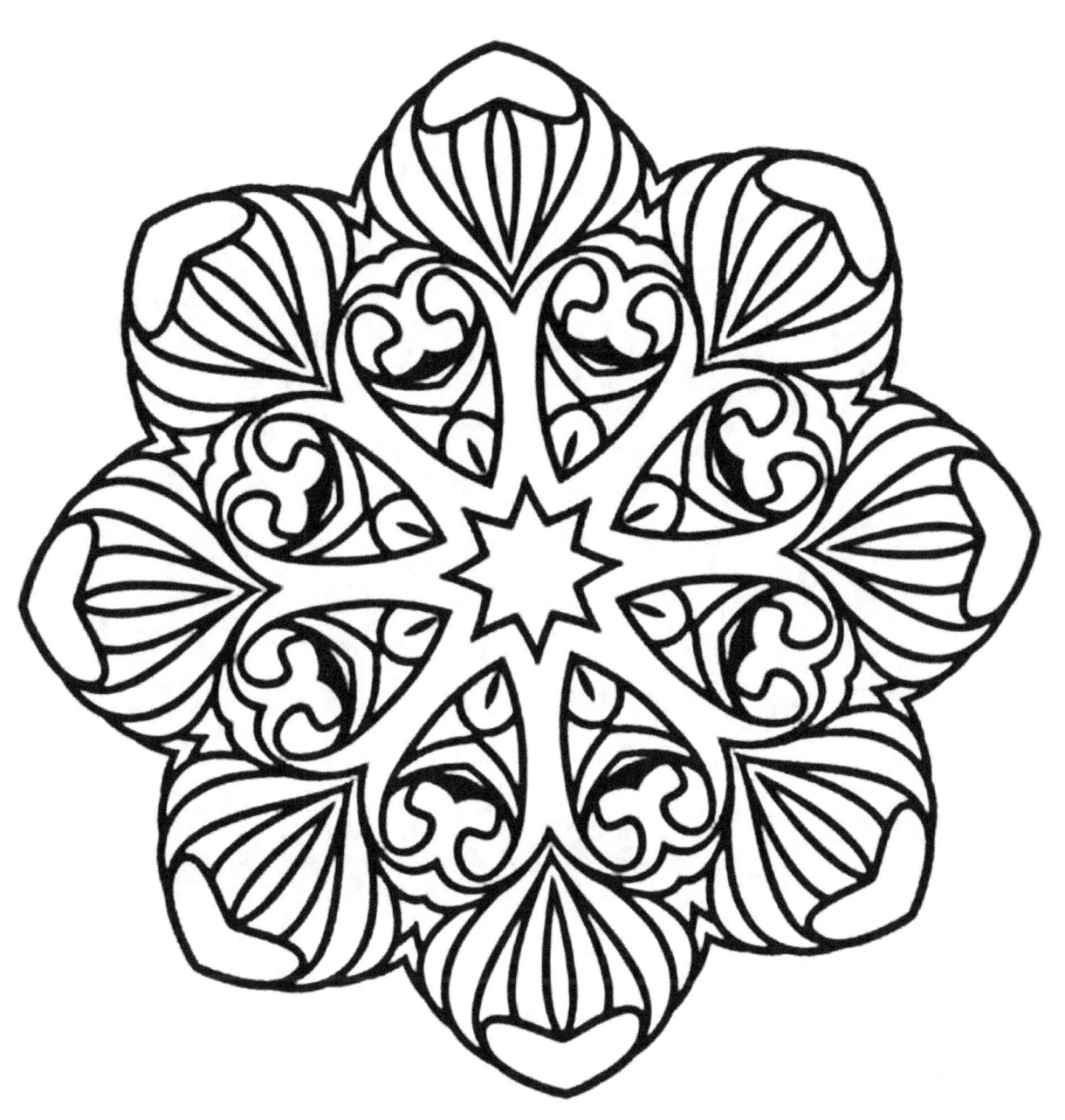

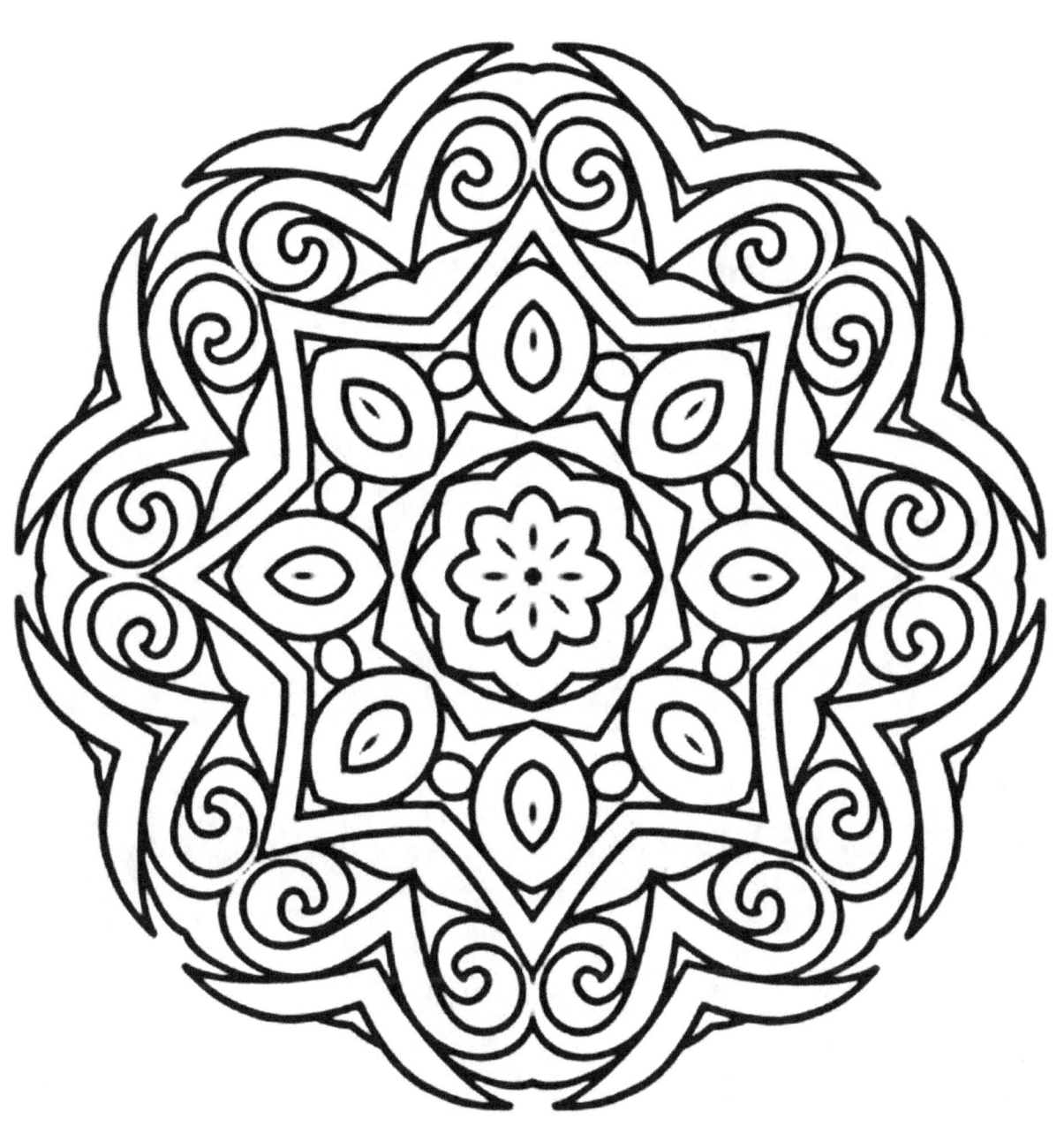

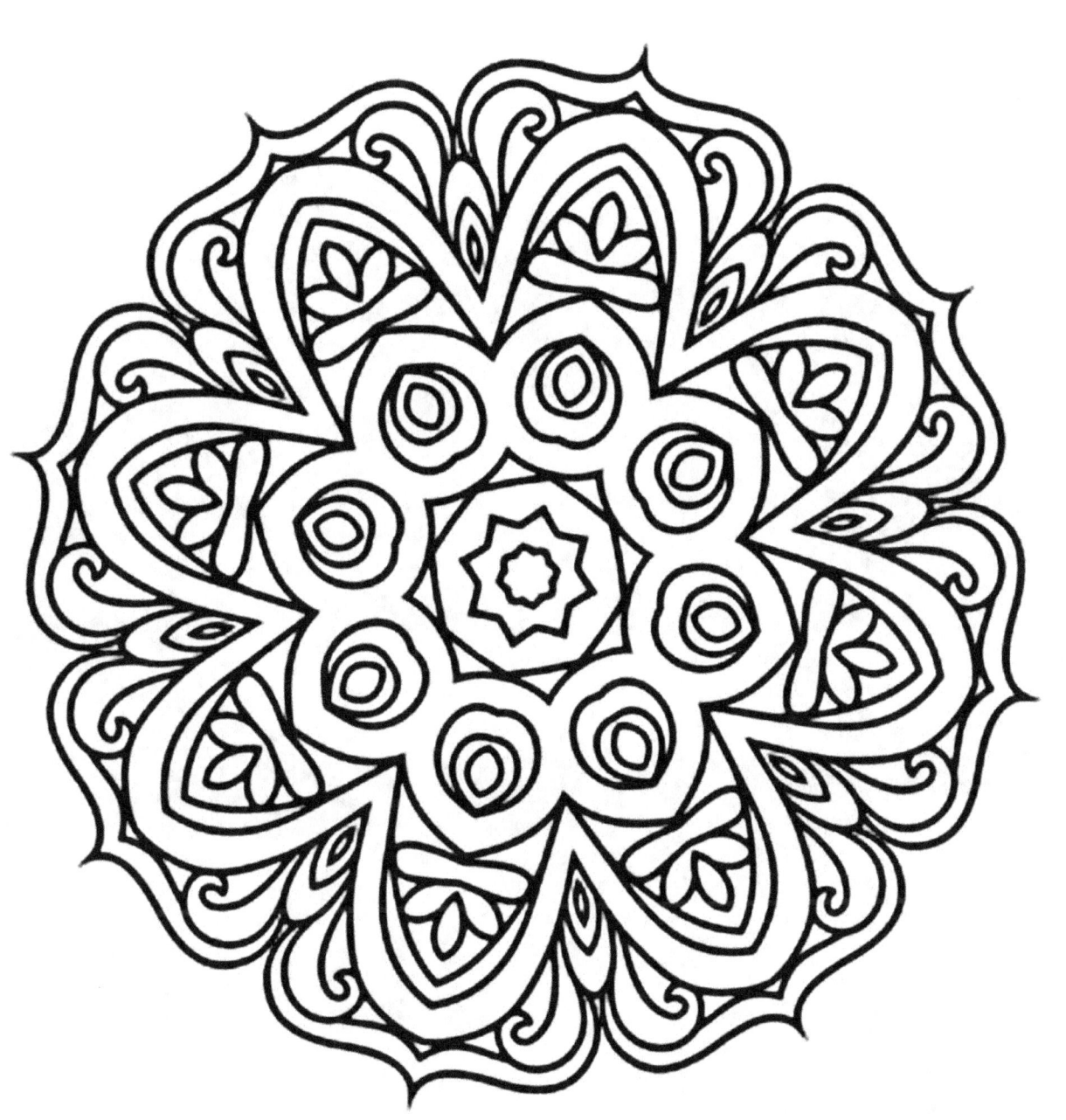

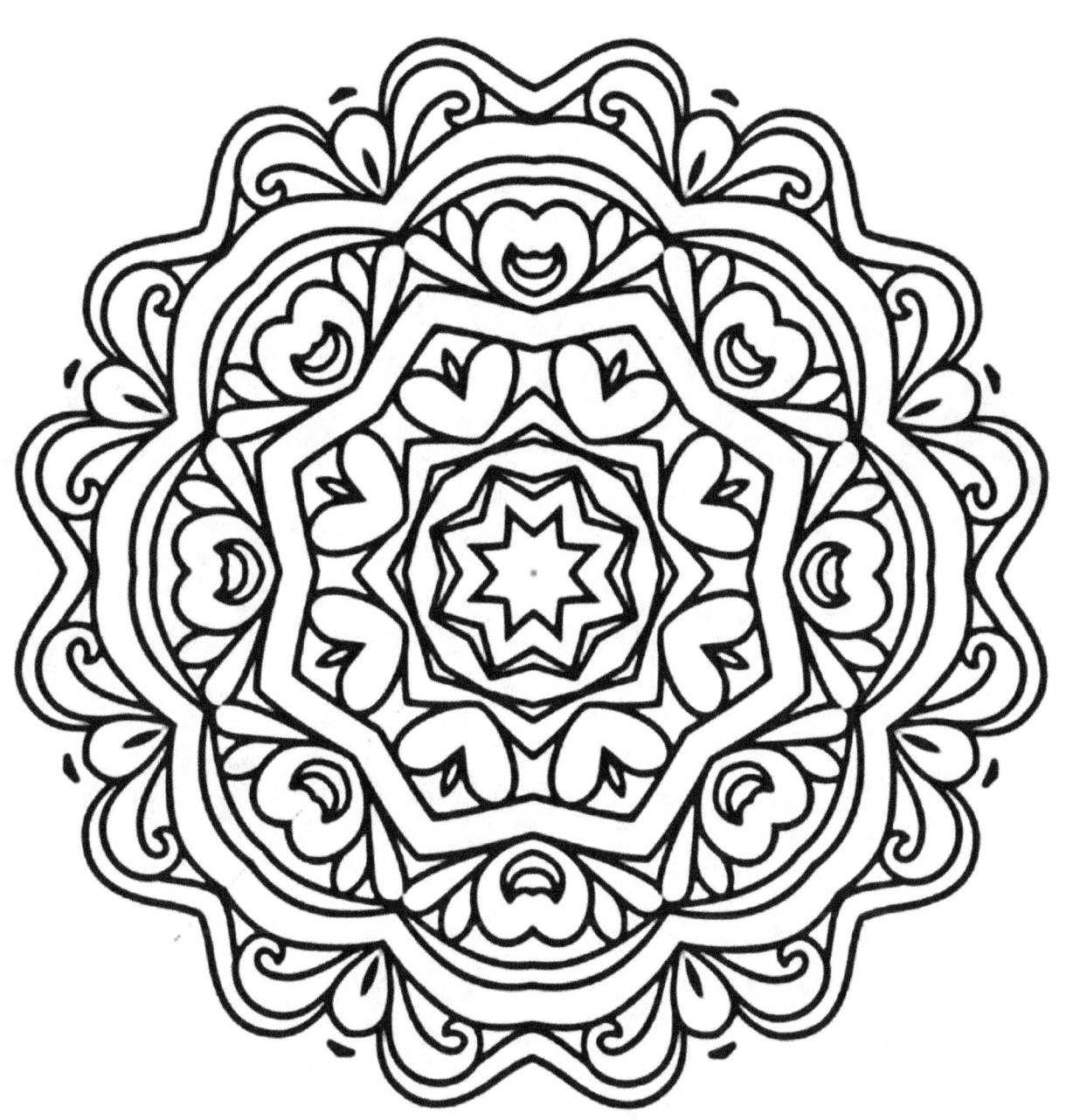

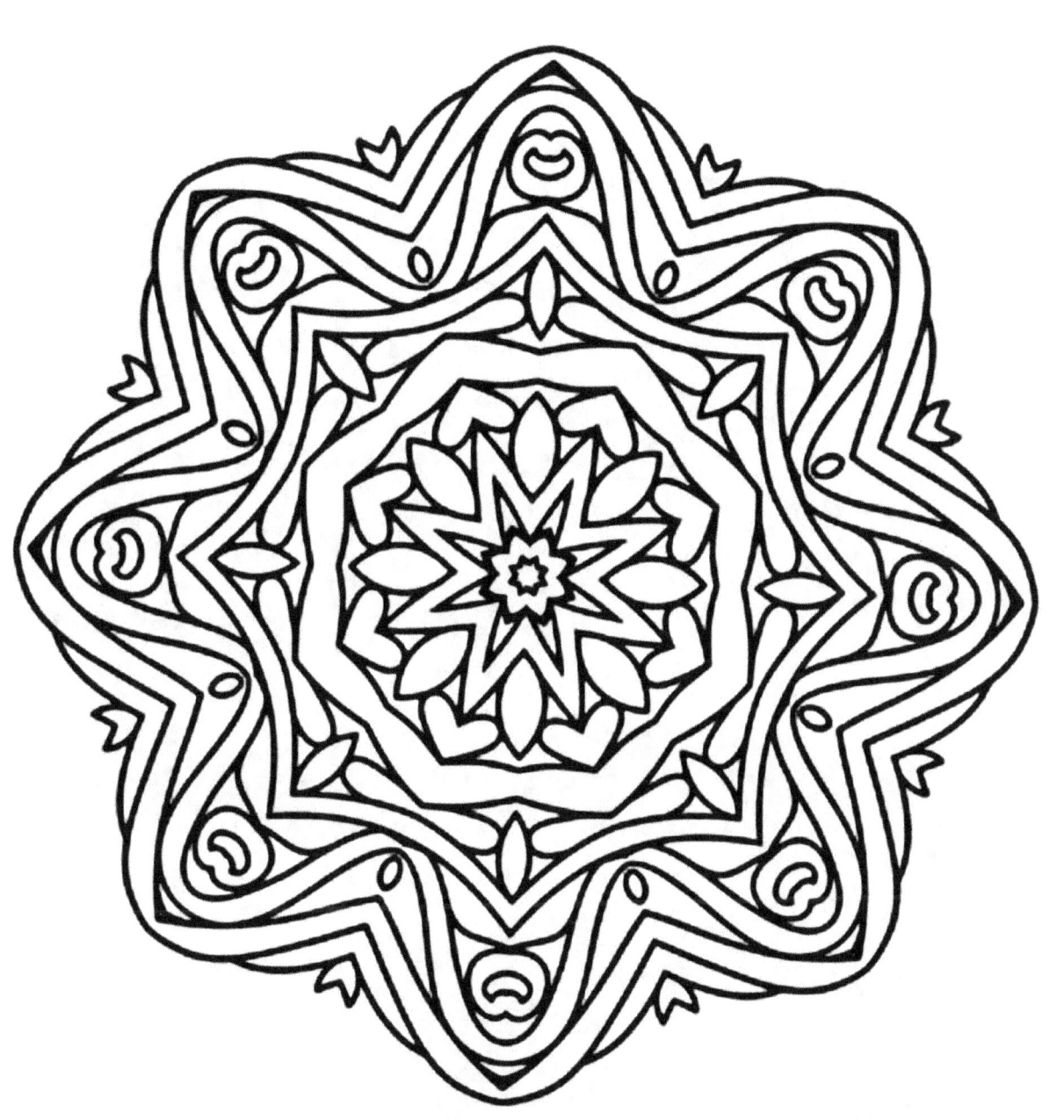

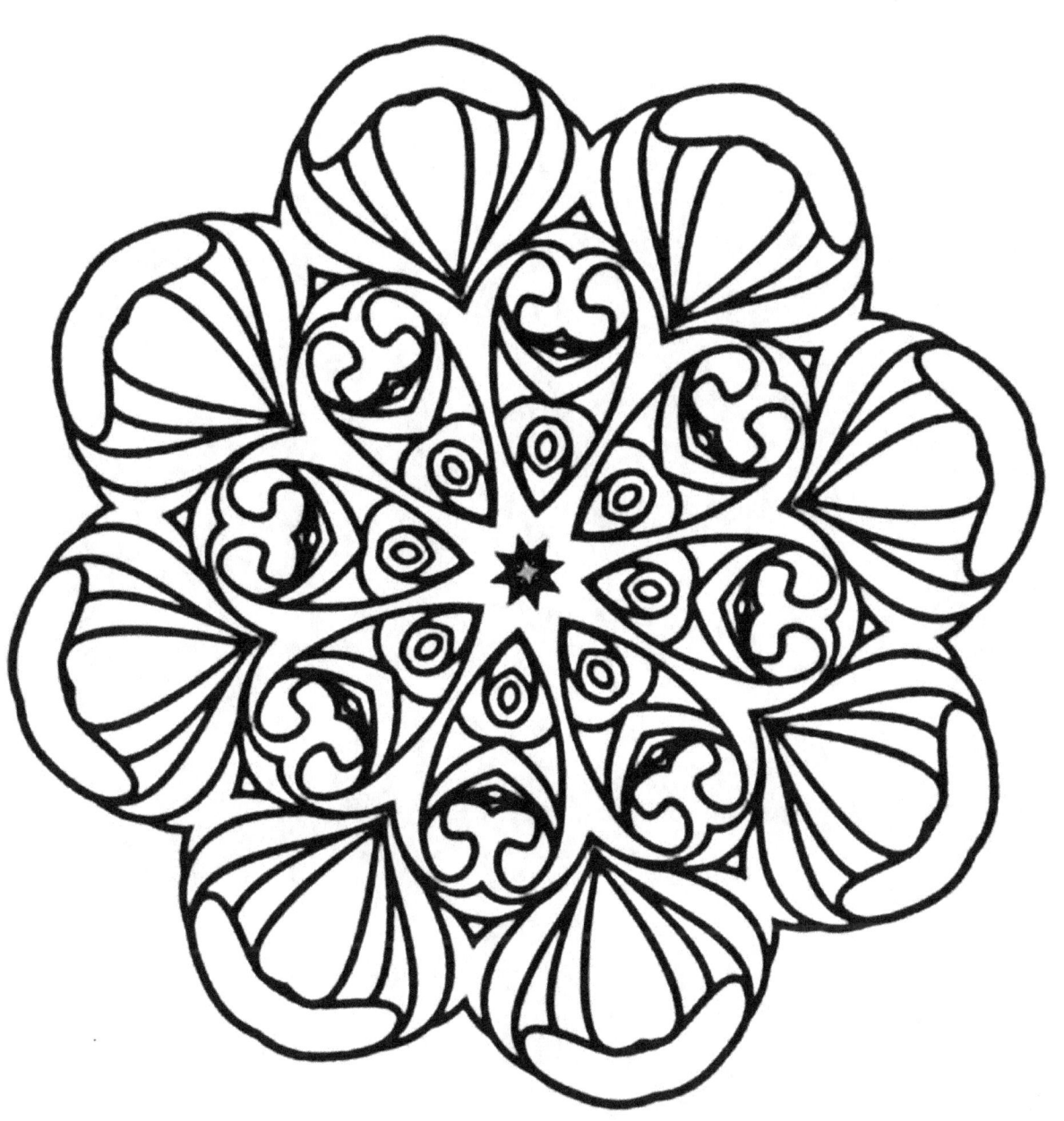

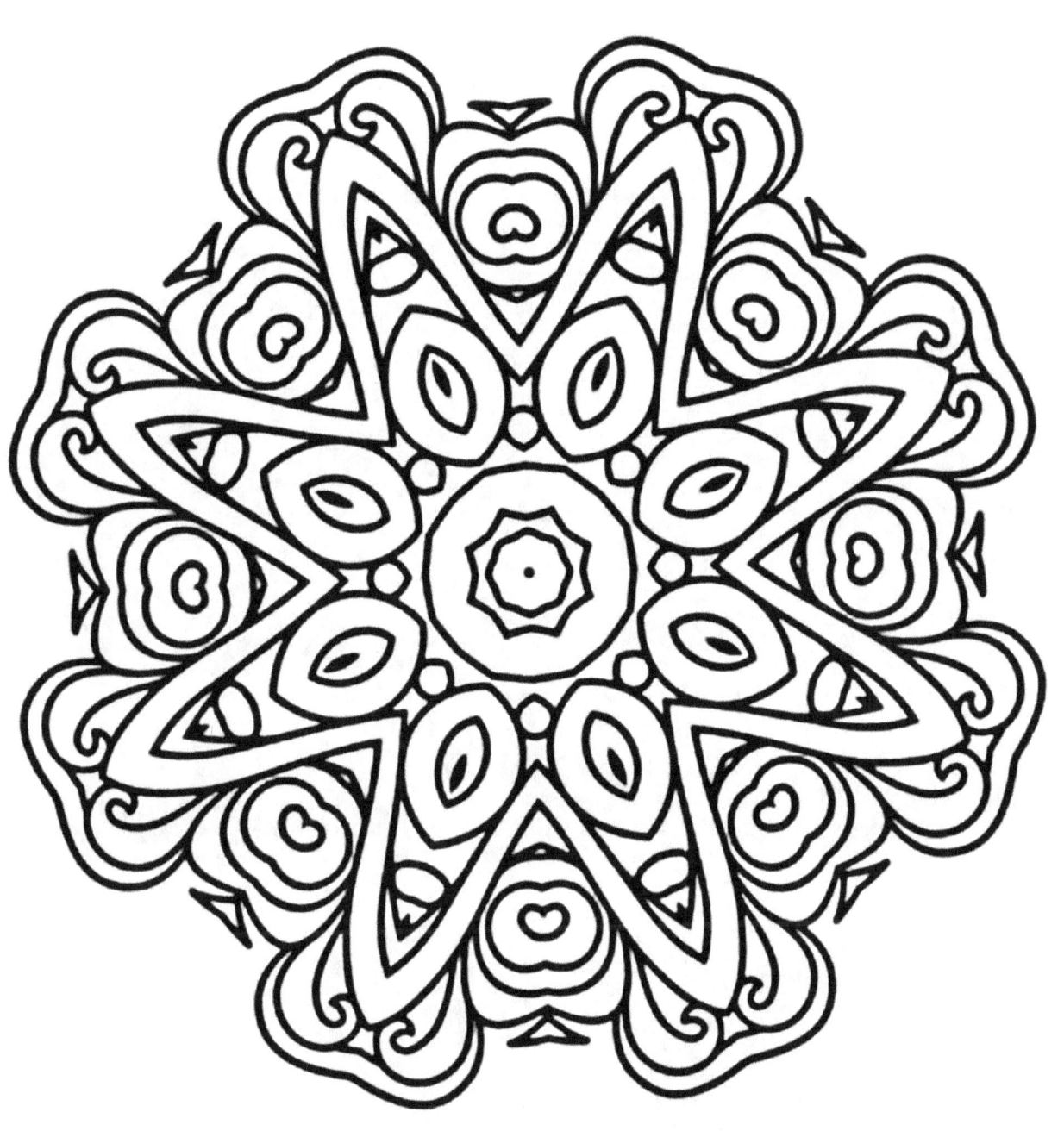

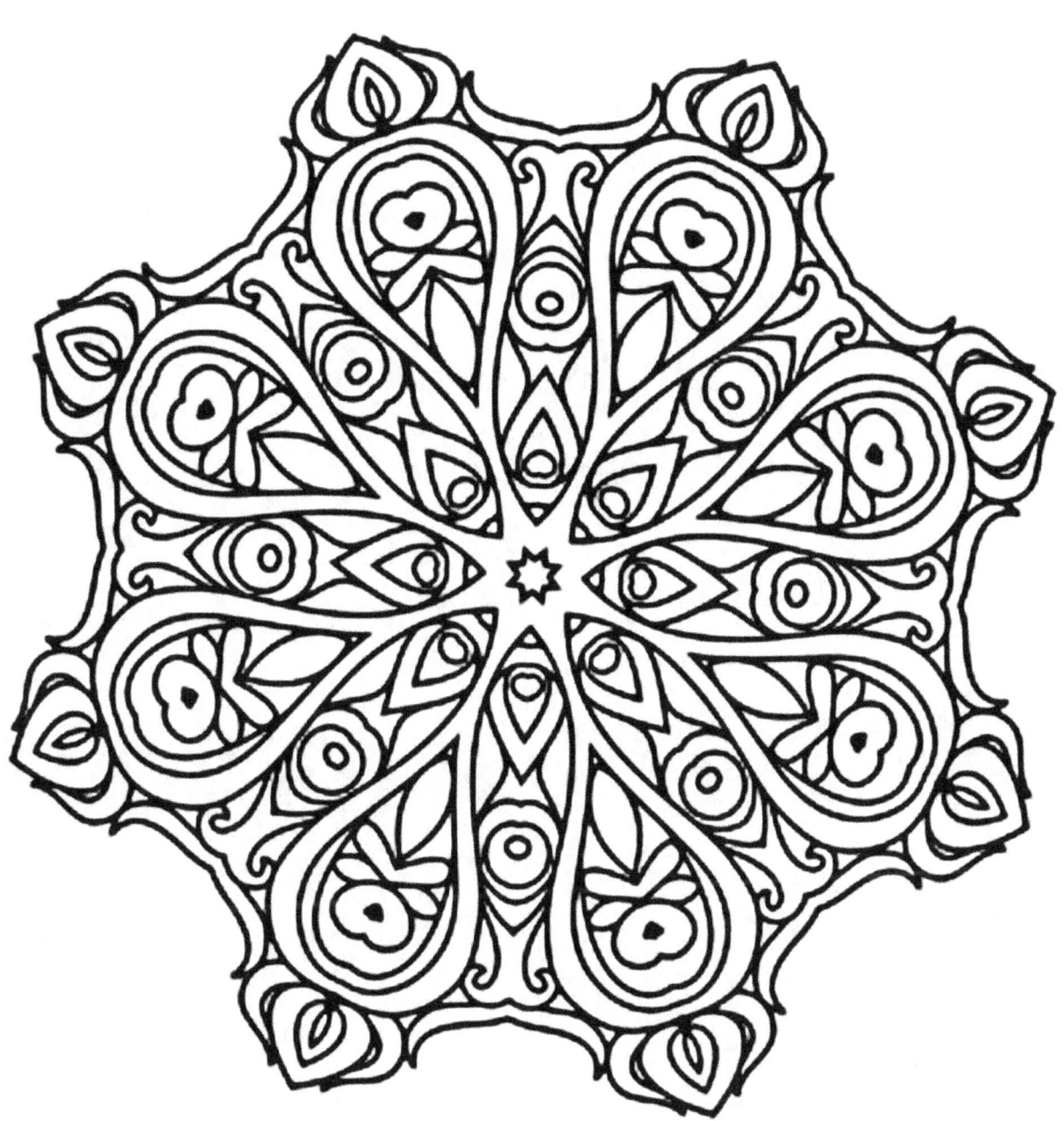

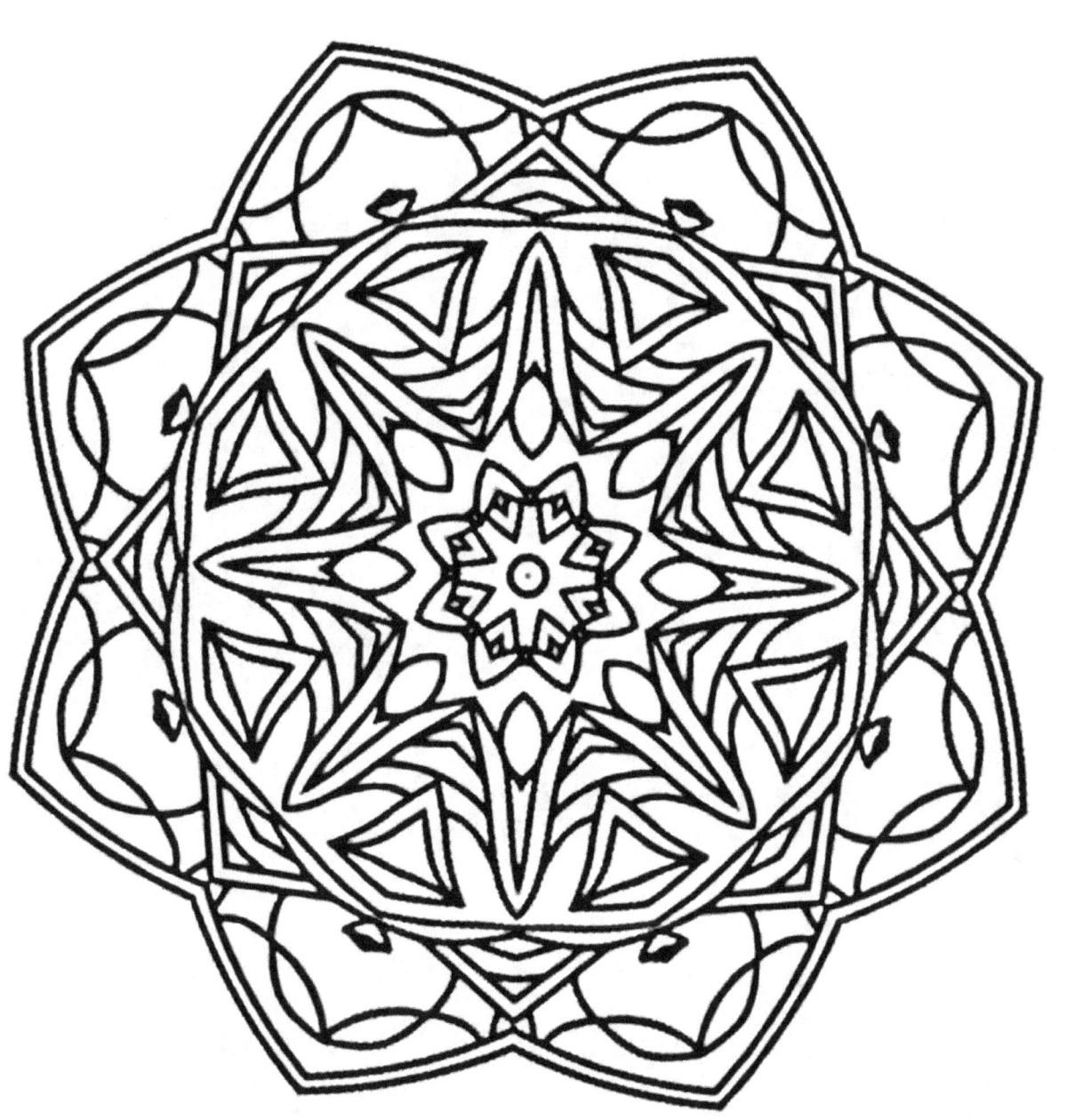

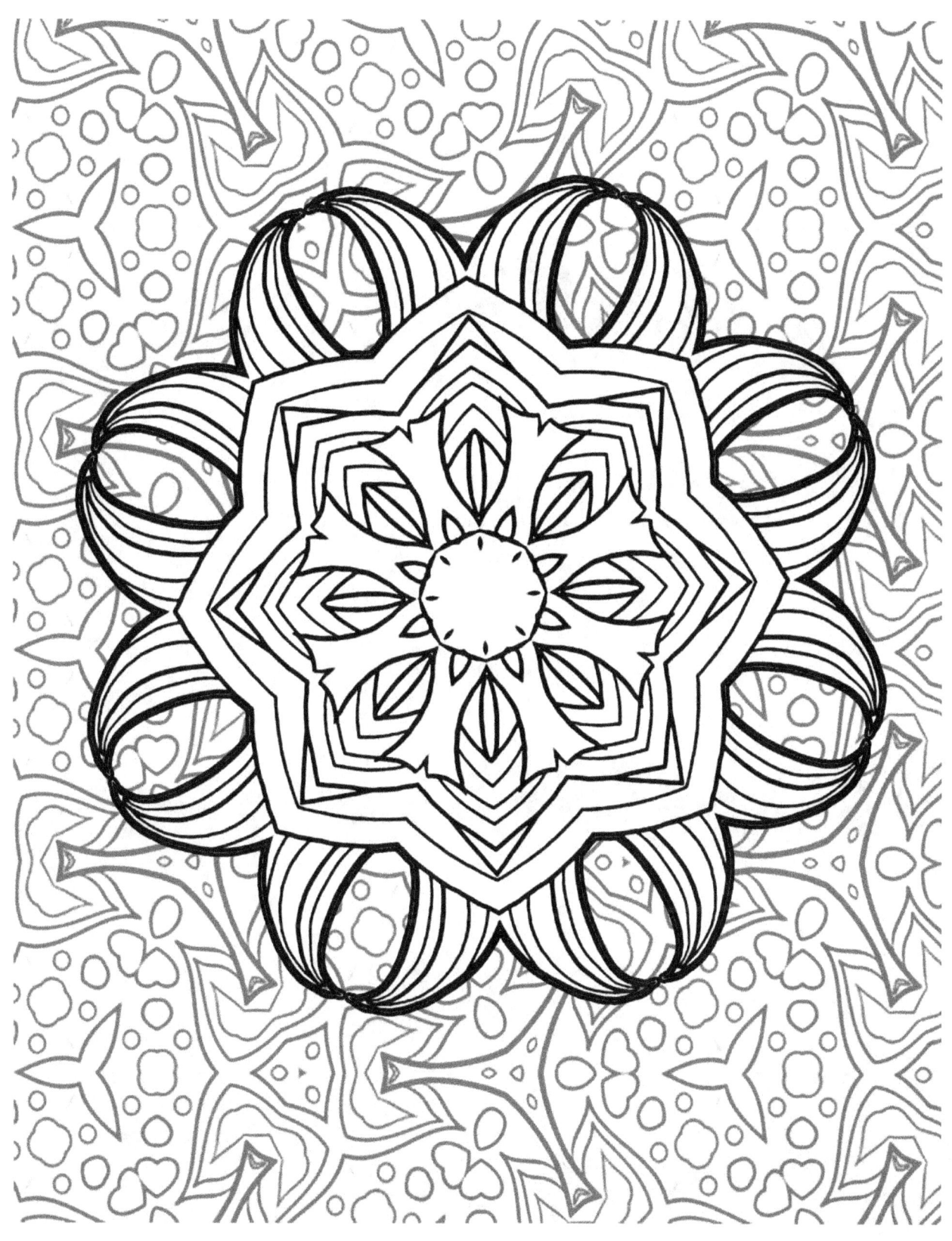

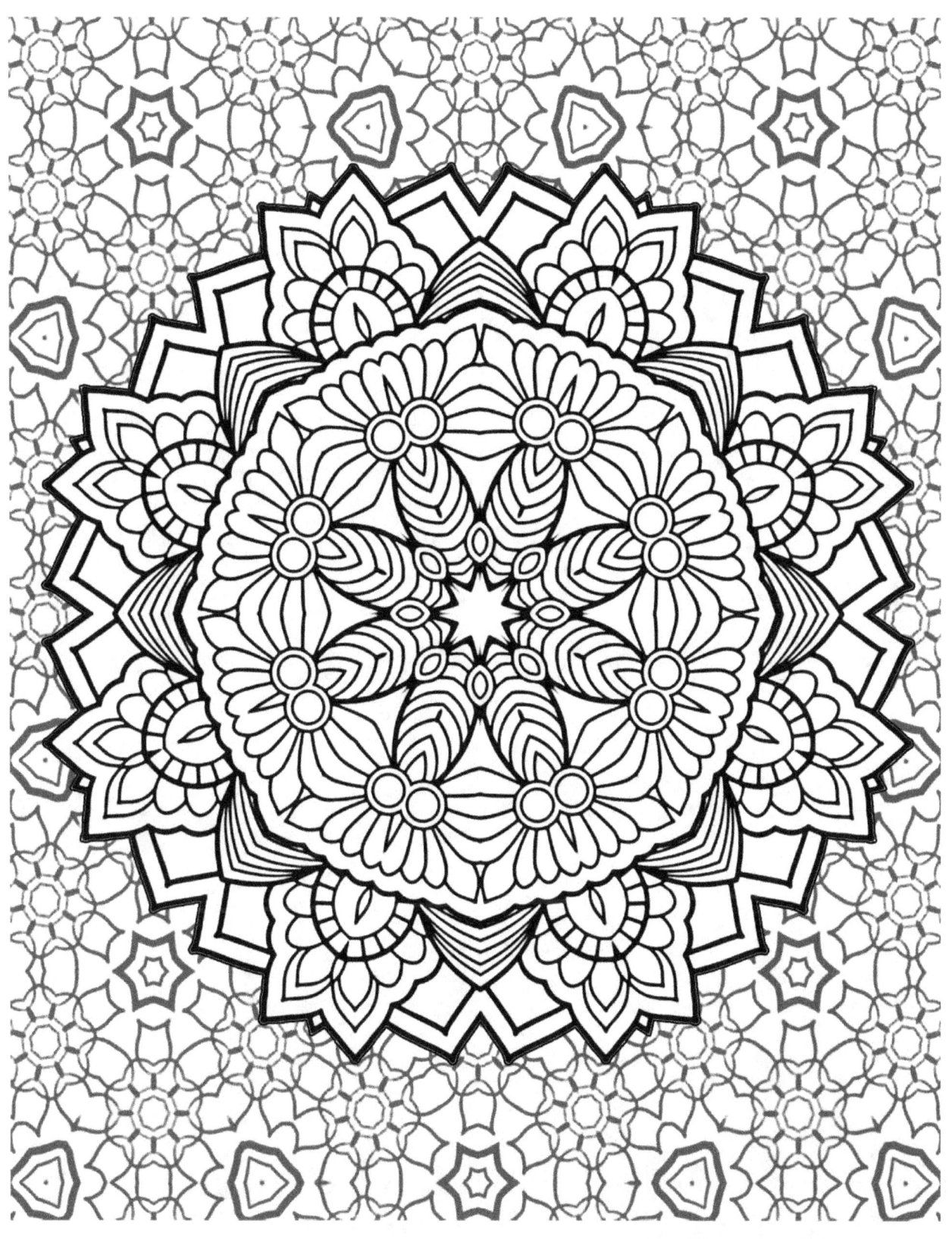

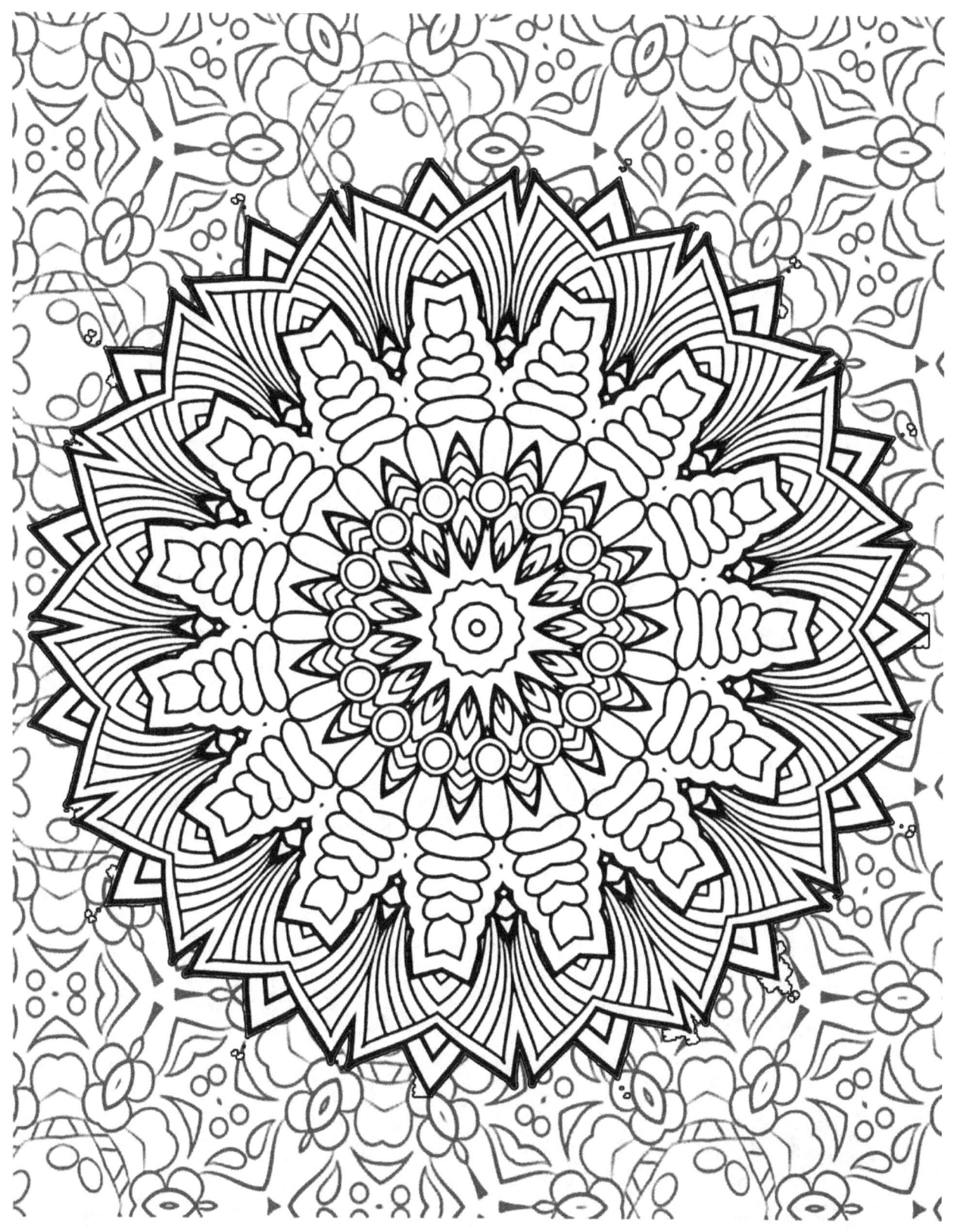

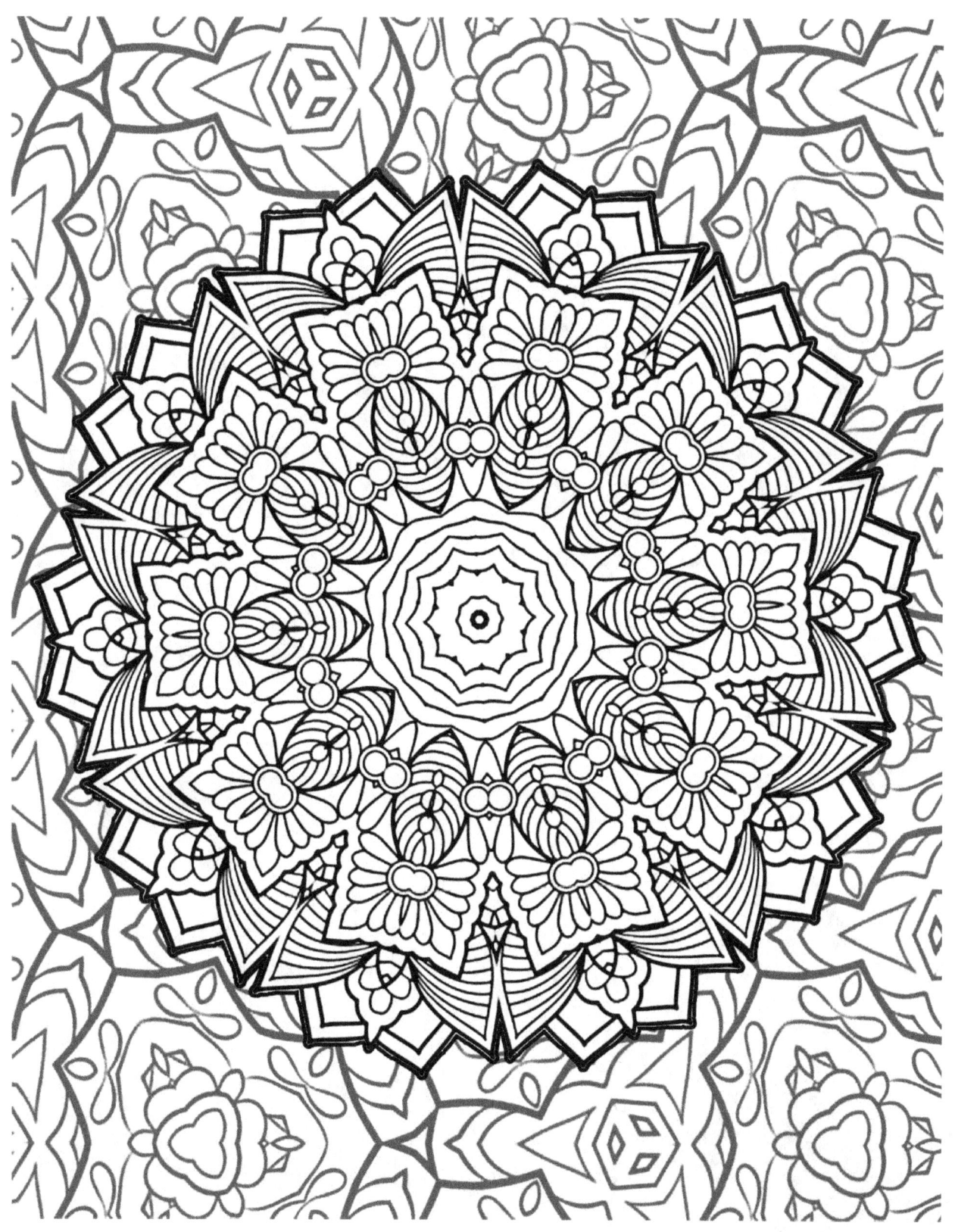

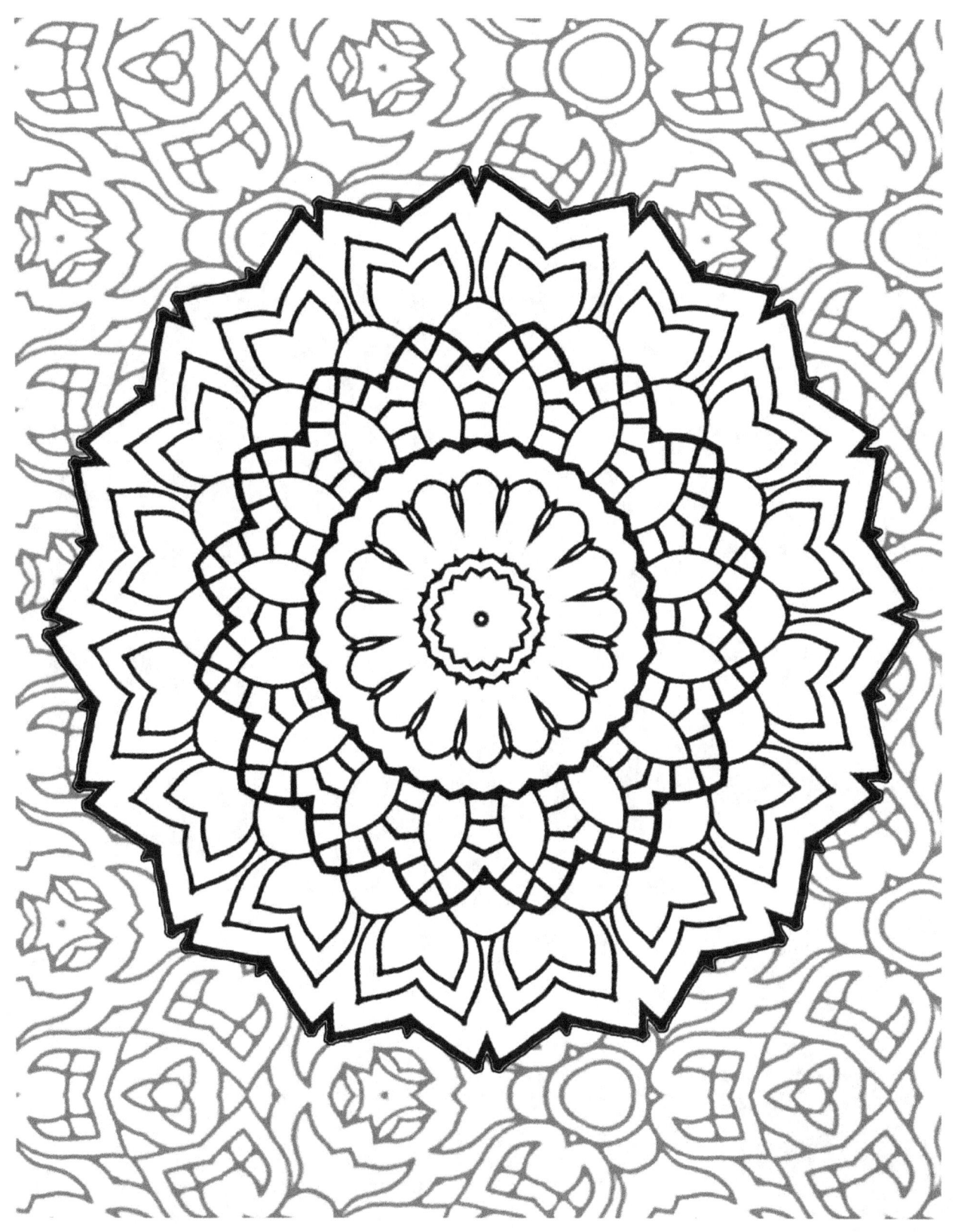

Thank you

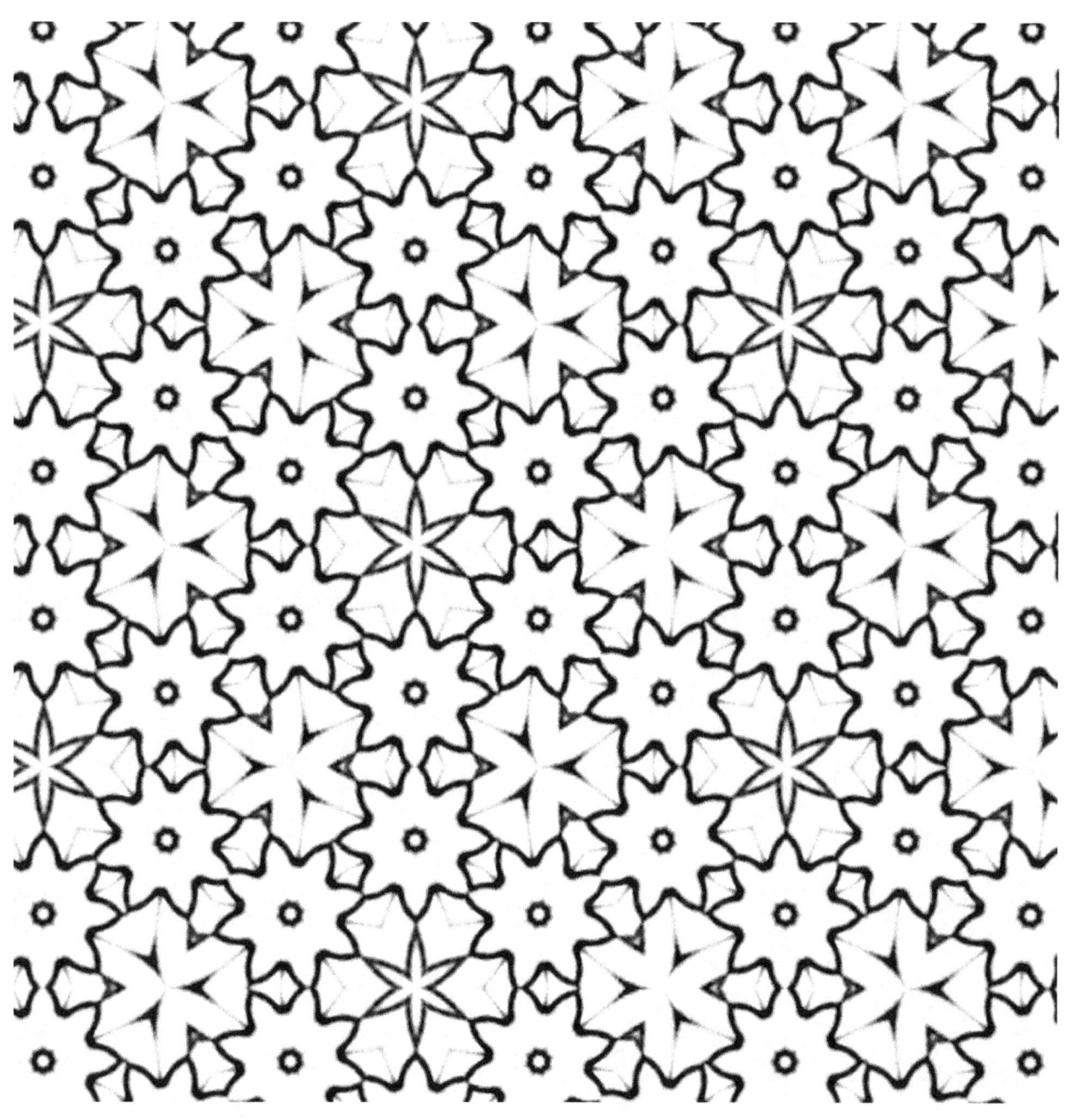

www.ingramcontent.com/pod-product-compliance
Lightning Source LLC
Chambersburg PA
CBHW081119180526
45170CB00008B/2923

9781544814858